CW00956719

SOHO PAST

First published 1994
by Historical Publications Ltd
32 Ellington Street, London N7 8PL
(Telephone 071-607 1628)

ISBN 0 948667 26 5
British Library Cataloguing-in-Publication Data.
A catalogue record for this book is available from the British Library.

Typeset in Palatino
by Historical Publications Ltd.
Reproduction by G & J Graphics, London EC1
Printed in Frome, Somerset by
Butler & Tanner

SOHO PAST

by
Richard Tames

with a concluding chapter by Bryan Burrough,
Chairman of the Soho Society

HISTORICAL PUBLICATIONS

Acknowledgments

Special thanks are due to the Soho Society, to the staff of the Museum of London, the Guildhall Library, the London Library and to John Sargent and Roy Harrison of the City of Westminster's Archives and Local History section, at present at the Victoria Library, Buckingham Palace Road. Acknowledgment is also made to the invaluable resource represented by the relevant volumes of the *Survey of London*, Judith Summers' *Soho* and Yves Jaulmes' research on the history of the Huguenot community.

The Illustrations

The Soho Society

The Soho Society is a Civic Trust Amenity Group which aims to make Soho a better place in which to live, work or visit. Details of membership may be obtained from the Society at St Anne's Tower, 55 Dean Street, W1V 5HH (071-439 4303).

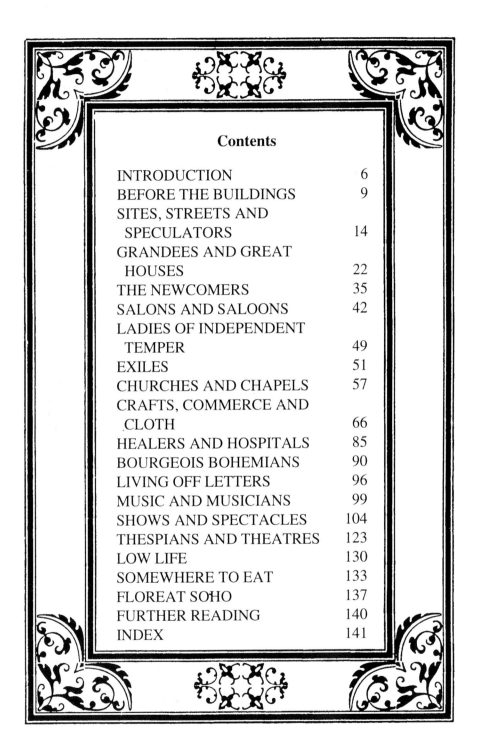

Contents

Introduction

Behind every door there is a story. Let one stand for all. What is now 12-13 Greek Street was originally a single building, the largest house in the street, known as Portland House and probably built by a glazier who lived at No. 17. Its first known occupant, in 1684, was Elizabeth Price, probably the actress and courtesan and she was succeeded in the following year by 'Lady Wolsingholm' and then by the French refugee, Abraham Meure, who turned the premises into a gentlemen's academy. Next came the Marquis of Trevi, the Sicilian ambassador and after him a former British ambassador to Savoy, William, later Viscount, Chetwynd, one of whose descendants would sponsor the building of 'model dwellings' in Soho in the following century. From 1744 to 1764 the occupant was Peter Legh, Esq. of Lyme Hall, Cheshire. After two years lying empty it was then taken over by one James Cullen, who was both an upholsterer and a

partner of the enterprising and colourful Mrs. Cornelys (see p104). Together they spent the not inconsiderable sum of £1,500 on 'Erecting different Buildings' at the back of the property, where they staged 'Assemblies', presumably as an overflow – or more discreet alternative – to the well-publicised shenanigans at Mrs. Cornelys' larger establishment in Soho Square. In 1773 the house was assessed for rates to the Hon. Baron Grant, not to be confused with the swindler of the same name who was to pay for the laying out of Leicester Square gardens exactly a century later.

In 1774 Josiah Wedgwood took over the premises as his London showrooms and presumably converted the outbuildings to provide his firm with 'Painting Shops, Stable, damaged ware room, Scowering room, retort room, Pearl ware room, Laboratory, Printing and Pattern rooms'. There is also an intriguing reference to a 'Chapel-Building, with Packing and un-

1. Nos. 12-13 Greek Street in 1914.

2. *Josiah Wedgwood.*

packing House' – perhaps a survival from the brief occupancy of the Sicilian envoy, who might have had a private place of worship similar to those tolerated for his counterparts from other Catholic states. With the Wedgwood firm's departure in 1797 fashionable status also gradually departed. A coachmaker's took over the premises, which were sub-divided soon after. Later occupants include the dramatist James Sheridan Knowles (1803-7), the sculptor William Cramphorn (1819) and the painters Robert Edmondstone (1833-4), William Barraud (1835-6) and John Lucas (1837). It was probably in 1846 that a passage-way was constructed between No. 12 and No. 13 to give access to the yard at the rear. The 1886 edition of Baedeker's guide to London recommends the restaurant at Wedde's Hotel, 12 Greek Street, no doubt because it was a 'German house'. Wedde's continued to occupy the premises until the outbreak of the Great War – when German names became unpopular. (It was at this time that the exclusive 'Coburg', named after the reigning dynasty, found it prudent to become the 'Connaught'.) The current food-establishments facing onto Greek Street, one Italian, one Mexican, therefore have a century of culinary tradition behind them. The backyard can similarly boast a commercial continuity. Formerly occupied by a timber merchant, it is now surrounded by handsome offices, brick-built, ivy-covered and, like the rest of Soho, sitting on a lot of history.

As it is of a house, so it is of a street.

Old Compton Street, originally Compton Street, is now Soho's High Street. Its first inhabitants, however, included a royal physician, a theologian, four ladies of title and a future vice-chamberlain to Queen Anne. A generation later the status of its inhabitants had moved decidedly down-market, though they were still respectable. About a third were French or of French origin, including the engraver Liart and ceramicist Sprimont. Later residents included the novelist John Cleland, the German scientist Friedrich Accum, the showman Wombwell, the classical architect Edward Inwood and no less than nineteen other known artists or engravers. Wagner lodged here for a week and the French poets Rimbaud and Verlaine were regular patrons of one of its pubs. By the 1790s, however, Old Compton Street's commercial character was already fairly established. Of its seventy-eight houses only seven or eight did not have shop-fronts and some of those were taverns.

Soho was the birth-place of William Beckford, the wealthiest man in eighteenth century England, and of William Blake, one of the most gifted. The poet Coventry Patmore grew up here and so did the entertainer, Jessie Matthews, whose father had a market stall. It has been home to Newton, Hogarth, Reynolds, Constable, Lawrence and Darwin, as well as to Casanova, Mozart and Karl Marx. Burke and Boswell sent their sons to be educated at the Soho Academy, which also numbered among its pupils the architect Philip Hardwick, the caricaturist Rowlandson and the painter Turner. Soho is the last resting-place of the ill-starred 'King of Corsica', of critic William Hazlitt and of Dorothy L. Sayers, translator of Dante and creator of Lord Peter Wimsey. Such rich literary associations are appropriate, for Soho as a location - romantic, exotic, seedy or plain squalid - has a secure place in the imaginative landscape of English fiction. Soho is the home of Sir Roger de Coverley in Thackeray's *Barry Lyndon* (1844). It also figures in Robert Louis Stevenson's *The Strange Case of Dr. Jekyll and Mr. Hyde* (1886), Joseph Conrad's *The Secret Agent* (1907), Michael Sadleir's *Fanny by Gaslight* (1940), P.D. James's *Unnatural Causes* (1967), John Fowles' *The French Lieutenant's Woman* (1969) and Timothy Mo's *Sour Sweet* (1982). Smollett had Matthew Bramble live in Golden Square, which was also the home of Ralph Nickleby and where Thackeray's hero, Henry Esmond, visits the snobbish General Webb. Manette Street (once Rose Street and traditionally pronounced Manetti by the Soho-born) commemorates the luckless Dr Manette of *A Tale of Two Cities*, while Mr. Jaggers, the lawyer in *Great Expectations*, inhabited Gerrard Street as the first-floor resident of a 'rather stately house of its kind, but dolefully in want of painting and with dirty windows'. Dickens' uncle did live in just such a house, at No. 10.

3. Old Compton Street in the 1920s.

Much fictional eating goes on in Soho. In G. K. Chesterton's *The Man Who Was Thursday* a band of anarchists meet on the balcony of a Leicester Square hotel for Sunday breakfast. John Galsworthy, creator of the conventionally-minded, upper middle class Forsyte dynasty, dined frequently in Soho - unlike the Forsytes:

'Of all quarters in the queer adventurous amalgam called London, Soho is perhaps the least suited to the Forsyte spirit. Untidy, full of Greeks, Ishmaelites, cats, Italians, tomatoes, restaurants, organs, coloured stuffs, queer names, people looking out of upper windows, it dwells remote from the British Body Politic.'

Initially developed as a residential area, Soho swiftly acquired a distinctly cosmopolitan character which it has never lost. Renowned for sex and catering in the twentieth century, it has also long been a significant manufacturing area. Once famed for guns, watches, violins and exquisite silverware, it also housed the mass-production of organs, billiard tables, paints, sheet music, tinplate, blacklead and pickles and in the present century has been responsible for the production of Sir Winston Churchill's birthday cakes, Fred Astaire's dancing shoes and Julie Andrews' wedding-dress.

Soho also has some claims as a birthplace of things that are writ large in the modern world: the world's first-ever public demonstration of television, by John Logie Baird, took place at 22 Frith Street on January

27th 1926; and an 'advertising contractor' put up his sign in Soho as early as 1869; Professor S.K. Uyenishi opened Britain's first 'judokan' – 'The School of Japanese Self Defence' – at 31 Golden Square in 1905; the Ford Motor Company, Pathe News, *Vogue* magazine and the British Board of Film Censors all had their first offices in Soho.

In recent years modernity, in the shape of property developers, has presented a more threatening guise - an ironic twist of history since Soho itself was virtually all built by speculators. Over a decade ago, in her magisterial guide to *The Art and Architecture of London*, Ann Saunders warned Soho saunterers:

' .... stand still and remember what you have seen, for the developers are moving in on Soho and no one can be certain how much longer this intriguing enclave will be with us... If Soho goes, the loss will be irreparable, for the survival of such an area, built between the late seventeenth and early nineteenth centuries and still with its original street pattern intact, is unique. Grander areas survive... but nowhere else in London is there quite the domestic simplicity, the humble but contented dignity, of these houses and shops, built on a modest, human scale, and still, for the most part, keeping to usages not so very far removed from their original purposes.'

Thanks to the valiant and imaginative efforts of the Soho Society the prospects for the area's active conservation as a true community seem much brighter now than when those words were written.

Before the buildings

BOUNDARIES

The area now loosely referred to as Soho comprises the parish of St Anne's and, from Wardour Street westwards, a northern part of the parish of St James's, Piccadilly. But, historically, Soho's boundaries have varied. Oxford Street has traditionally defined its northern edge, but inhabitants of Fitzrovia have periodically referred to their district as 'North Soho', a designation indignantly rejected by inhabitants of Soho proper.

The western boundary – Regent Street – dates from the 1820s and its construction necessarily entailed a process of territorial adjustment. George IV's compliant instrument, John Nash, fully intended to construct a frontier between the glitterati of Mayfair and the literati – and other less glamorous inhabitants – of Soho. Aiming to produce as far as possible 'a complete separation between the Streets occupied by the Nobility and Gentry, and the narrower Streets and meaner houses occupied by mechanics and the trad-

ing part of the community', Nash designed his new street so that it would 'cross the eastern entrance to all the streets occupied by the higher classes and to leave out to the east all the bad streets...'. Soho may be grateful for Nash's unflinching snobbery. He established a boundary so unambiguous that it has helped to preserve Soho's village atmosphere from invasion ever since.

The eastern boundary is now marked by Charing Cross Road, but this thoroughfare only dates from the 1880s. Like Shaftesbury Avenue, which bisects Soho diagonally, it is a product of the efforts of the Metropolitan Board of Works to ease the capital's traffic flow while simultaneously demolishing some of its worst slum housing. Charing Cross Road, as far as Cambridge Circus, followed the line of Hog Lane, but south of that carved brutally through a maze of short streets and courts, isolating to the east a small portion of St Anne's Parish which has, for the purposes of this book, been omitted.

Soho's southern boundary likewise now follows no neat line and has therefore, for convenience, been taken to embrace the south side of Leicester Square and the streets immediately adjacent to it.

4. *The so-called 'Agas' view of London in the 1550s. This extract shows Charing Cross at the bottom of the picture, south of today's Trafalgar Square. St Martin's Lane stretches north by the side of St Martin-in-the-Fields, and Hedge Lane is roughly today's Haymarket. In between these roads lies the agricultural area which was to become Soho.*

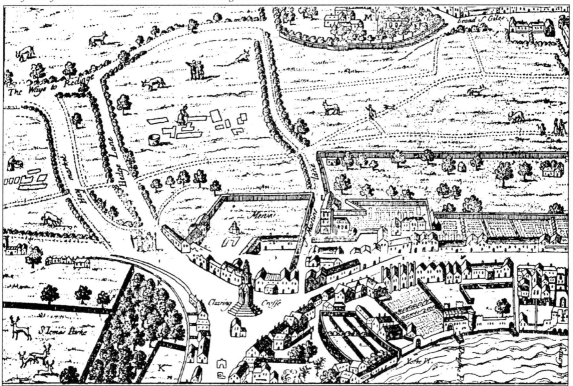

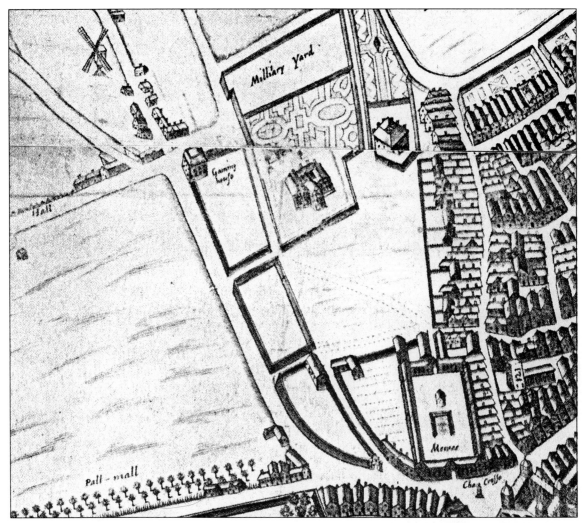

5. *Extract from the Newcourt and Faithorne map of c1658. Buildings, shown again in Illustration 7, have appeared on the Soho fields. As with Illustration 4, Charing Cross is to the south of the map. The Royal Mews, where the sovereign's horses were kept, is on the site of the National Gallery.*

Originally all this land belonged to Westminster Abbey, which leased it to the Mercers' Company of the City of London, the Abbey of Abingdon and the Hospital of Burton Saint Lazar, while local people retained customary rights to dry clothes and graze cattle there after the summer hay-cut. Following the dissolution of the monasteries the area passed to the Crown and was subsequently redistributed piecemeal over the following century and a half into private ownership to make a patchwork of estates, some scattered, some compact, whose ownership very largely determined the street-lines of Soho as it is today.

BUILDING

Soho probably takes its name from an ancient hunting cry, indicating sight of the prey. It is certainly known that the Lord Mayor of London and his retinue traversed the area in September 1562 to inspect the waterworks at Stratford Place off Oxford Street and the conduits which contributed to the City's water-supply and that, in the course of their expedition, they hunted and feasted in the area, thus combining business with pleasure – very much a later Soho tradition.

A plan of 1585 shows that Soho was still almost entirely free of buildings, beyond a dozen or so scattered houses of a very humble character. Technically, building within three miles of the City of London was prohibited by royal decree. In practice the Crown's

6. *Part of the City of London's water supply was carried from the springs at Paddington and by today's Stratford Place, through Soho down to Fleet Street. These elm conduit pipes, outside St Anne's church, were laid bare during the construction of Shaftesbury Avenue in the 1880s and were probably part of that supply line.*

need for money led it to undermine its own authority by granting exemptions, formally or otherwise, to the influential and the wealthy.

Sometimes construction could be justified in terms of public policy. This certainly seems to have been the case in 1615 when a 'Military Company' was established in Westminster and, encouraged by the Crown via the Privy Council, acquired three and a half acres in the north-west part of 'St. Martin's Field' as an exercise ground. In 1616 the area was surrounded by a brick wall nine feet high which protected a two-storey brick 'Armoury House', with a tile roof. Over a hundred feet long and about a third as wide, this housed a large hall – to serve as a fencing salle, gymnasium and banquet-house – a library, a meeting-cum-dining room and kitchen. The furnishings included tables, four dozen leather chairs, a carved and gilded royal coat of arms, a chained Bible, a large iron grate which ran on wheels, painted candle-holders and several 'Statues of Emperors' heads, as well as quantities of arms, armour and ammunition.

Apart from training its own members the Company also appears to have acted as a force of special constables on Shrove Tuesday, when apprentices were by tradition allowed to get a bit out of hand - but not too much. What the Military Company did during the

7. The Military Yard and its buildings in the 'north-west part of St Martin's Field', just south of today's Oxford Street.

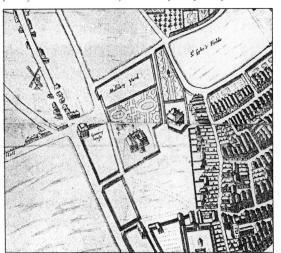

Civil Wars is unknown; if, indeed, it functioned as a unit, which seems improbable, given the opportunities for command in the scratch armies on both sides for any man with a plausible claim to military training. By 1656, however, the Company as a corporation was indisputably in debt and the rates on its house and grounds were being paid by a cook and a gardener, presumably employees who had been charged with their safekeeping. In 1661 the cook and a number of members of the Company were paid £500 for their interests in the premises by the ferocious Colonel Charles Gerard - of whom more anon.

Immediately adjacent to the Military Ground on its western boundary was a gaming house to which the members of the Company no doubt gave much custom. Erected around 1634 by Simon Osbaldeston, barber to the Lord Chamberlain, it was an elegant and imposing building. As early as 1636 it earned itself a highly appropriate nickname after Lord Dunbar lost £3,000 at a sitting – 'Shaver's Hall'. The building was subsequently occupied by Henry Coventry, Secretary of State 1672-79, whose occupation is memorialised in the name of Coventry Street.

In 1650 the only significant cluster of buildings in the Soho area was along the line of what is now Wardour Street and was then Colman Hedge Lane. There were reckoned to be over sixty, but with the exception of four three-storey brick houses, almost all the rest were 'Cottages... Shedds or meane habitacons'. Yet, just over twenty years later, a Secretary of State was living a few hundred yards away. What had happened?

What had happened was the Great Fire of 1666, which burned out some 13,000 houses and rendered 100,000 of the kingdom's better-off citizens homeless. Dispossessed Londoners looked for somewhere new to live and the grazing fields west of the City and north of Westminster looked a good deal more attractive than the raggle-taggle wasteland, disfigured by rubbish-dumps, cow-byres, shipyards, rope-walks and filthy industrial premises which were already giving Tower Hamlets an unenviable character. Even more to the point, the land to the north-west of St Martin-in-the-Fields was within easy reach of the three royal palaces at Westminster, Whitehall and St James's – and much of it was still in the gift of a dynasty none too securely reunited with its throne. Soho was on the way up – for a while.

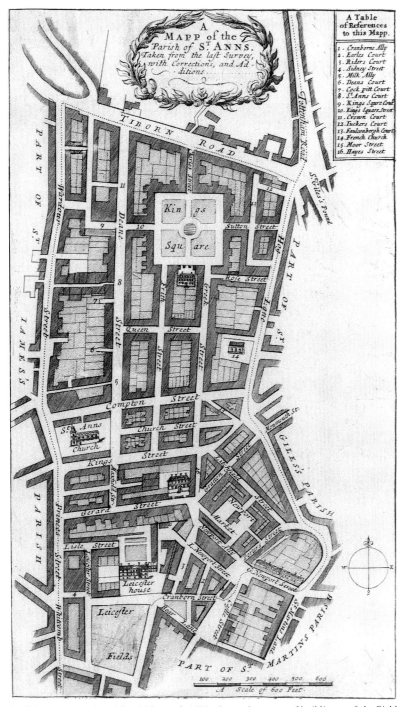

8. Soho transformed. This parish map by Richard Blome of c1690, shows the extent of building on Soho Fields after the Great Fire had destroyed much of the City of London. King's Square was the original name of Soho Square, and the Tiborn Road above it is today's Oxford Street. A prominent feature to the south-east is Newport Market, its form still recognisable in the present street pattern.

9. *Golden Square looking north in 1754; by Sutton Nicholls.*

Sites, Streets and Speculators

A MATTER OF STREET NAMES

The names of Soho's streets reflect its builders, what they built on, what they did there, whom they admired, or thought could be useful to them.

Golden Square, begun in 1674, was from the outset intended for 'such houses as might accommodate Gentry', so the familiar, but indelicate name by which the area was known – Gelding Close – had to go. By the time its first residents moved in, the more refined corruption was already in use.

Great Windmill Street was a footpath in Tudor times, leading through Windmill Field to a tall, brick-

finished, Time will make appear.' His scepticism was fully justified: intended to rival the more famous Haymarket a few hundred yards to the south, it failed to fulfil its destiny and today is occupied by public conveniences. The handsome terrace of six houses (nos. 48-58) on the north side dates from 1722-3. Charles Bridgman, the celebrated landscape gardener, occupied No. 54 from 1723 to 1738.

In late Stuart London the agrarian and the industrial co-existed. Brewer Street takes its name from two breweries which once stood along its northern side. The first, opened in 1664, belonged to Thomas Ayres (hence nearby Air Street) and continued brewing until 1826 – Lex Garage now occupies its site. Davies's brewery adjoined it on the west and lasted from 1671 to the 1740s.

Glasshouse Street, another Tudor cart track, was leased in 1675 to Windsor Sandys who supplied the Glass Sellers' Company and also had the contract to remove night-soil from the parishes of St Giles-in-the-Fields and St Martin-in-the-Fields. Since saltpetre is both a by-product of night-soil and used in the making of glass Sandys intertwined his business interests. Certainly one business is the derivation of Glasshouse Street, and perhaps the other may have given rise to Peter Street.

ROYAL CONNECTIONS

Kingly Street was King Street until 1906, when the suffix was added to distinguish it from other King Streets. It was once a footpath across Six Acre Close and dubbed King Street when the path was widened in 1686, either as a compliment to the recent accession of James II or more simply because the land over which it passed had originally been acquired from the Church by Henry VIII.

Rupert Street, laid out in 1676, compliments Prince Rupert of the Rhine, inventor, dashing Royalist commander of the civil wars and subsequently naval hero of the Anglo-Dutch conflict.

Old Compton Street was simply Compton Street until the 1820s. Rapidly built up between 1677 and 1683, its name derives from Henry Compton, Bishop of London, who throughout that period was fundraising for the projected Soho parish church which he dedicated as St Anne's in 1686. Nearby Dean Street is probably named in recognition of the same prelate's position as Dean of the Chapel Royal.

Berwick Street betrays completely opposite sympathies. Laid out in the turbulent years 1688-9 by a Catholic, James Pollett, it is named after his patron, the Duke of Berwick, bastard son of James II, then fighting in Ireland to retrieve his father's lost throne.

Poland Street, begun in 1689, honours John Sobieski, ruler of Poland, whose dramatic intervention at the siege of Vienna in 1683 freed all Europe from the menace of Ottoman conquest.

built windmill, built around 1560, on the site of Ham Yard, opposite where the Windmill Theatre now stands. Clearly marked as a local landmark on maps of the area for over a century, the windmill had gone by the 1690s.

Broadwick Street was Broad Street until 1936, when the 'wick' was added to distinguish it from other streets of the same name. Its old name was entirely accurate because it was laid out in 1686 to be exceptionally wide. Strype, writing around 1720, observed that 'About the Middle of this Street is a Place designed for a Hay Market... but whether it will be

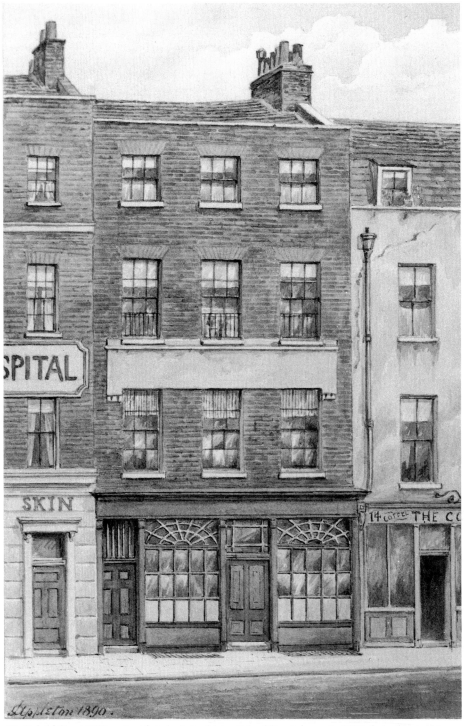

10. *Poland Street 1890, watercolour by J. Appleton. Poland Street, begun in 1689, derived its name from John Sobieski, the 17th-century ruler of Poland.*

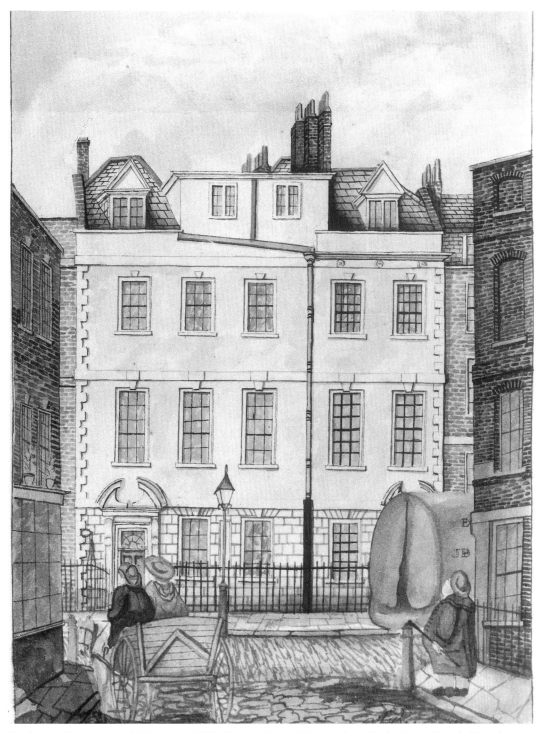

11. *Gerrard Street, from a sketch taken in 1826. The street derived its name from Charles, Baron Gerard of Brandon, Suffolk.*

Great Marlborough Street acclaims a national idol of almost royal status and was the first in London to do so, being laid out in 1704, the year of Marlborough's spectacular victory over the armies of Louis XIV at Blenheim. Nearby Ramillies Street and Place, honouring his victory of 1706, were known as Blenheim Street until 1885.

MISCELLANEOUS DEVELOPERS

Charles, Baron Gerard of Brandon in Suffolk (later first Earl of Macclesfield) and Colonel of the 1st Life Guards, set a high-handed example of how to deal with land ownership disputes, when in 1661 he seized the old military exercise yard and, backed by a ruffianly band of ex-servicemen, threatened to 'Cutt the Members of the said Millitary Company in peeces, if ever they came on the said Ground'. Some twenty years later the building of Gerrard Street was undertaken on his behalf by Dr Nicholas Barbon, the most notoriously unscrupulous, and successful, property developer of his day. Barbon's usual method was to build as quickly as possible, as cheaply as possible and preferably with someone else's money.

The origins of Panton Square (now demolished) and Panton Street are only slightly more respectable. Col. Thomas Panton, a card-sharp of legendary prowess, is said to have quit gambling for good after winning enough in a single night to bring him an annual income of £1,500. Instead he took to gambling of a different kind, laying out the square and street named for him; in his building petition to the king he enlisted Sir Christopher Wren to swear that the new thoroughfare would 'ease in some measure the great passage of the Strand, and will cure the noysomeness of that part'.

If Panton can be said to have risen without trace the Pulteneys could boast a far longer local pedigree. As early as 1575 a Thomas Pulteney was farming a number of scattered fields in the areas which became Mayfair, St James's Park and Soho. His successor, another Thomas, enclosed local common land and threatened 'death to any that shall presume to open the same'. As the westward march of the capital's expansion raised the value of the land in its path all the Pulteneys had to do was wait. In 1808 the Pulteney estate passed to Sir Richard Sutton, a descendant of Baron Lexington – hence Sutton Court and Lexington Street.

Commercial acumen also featured in the lands acquired and developed by Sir Robert Baker and his quarrelsome descendants. A successful tailor who made a fortune out of 'pickadills', a fashionable border for ruffs and collars, Baker turned landowner around 1612, buying up plots of land and building himself a mansion which his aristocratic neighbours sneeringly referred to as 'Pickadill Hall' - from which

Piccadilly takes its name. Baker died in 1623 and so did his children and grandchildren within a few years thereafter, leaving more distant relatives to squabble over the inheritance – notably his son-in-law, Sir Henry Oxenden and his great-nephews, John and James Baker. Sir Henry eventually grabbed Scavenger's Close (an apt name in the circumstances) and turned it into Oxendon Street. John and James meanwhile fell out over the disposition of Gelding Close. James employed a carpenter, Axtell, also named James, to build on one side of the field, hence Upper and Lower James Street. John employed a bricklayer, Emlyn, also named John, to build on the other, hence Upper and Lower John Street.

If John and James Street constitute a double echo then Sherwood Street is a corrupted one, for its creator was Francis Sherard. He began to build a number of expensive houses in this area around 1670 but died ten years later, heavily indebted. His family did, however, ultimately benefit from his efforts until his lease expired in 1821.

Beak Street was initially developed around 1680 by Thomas Beake, who subsequently became one of Queen Anne's Messengers.

Wardour Street illustrates how courtiers and craftsmen could work in partnership. An ancient trackway, it was once known as Colman Hedge Lane, taking its name from Colman Hedge Close, of which it formed one boundary. In 1631 this parcel of land was acquired by Sir Edward Wardour, an Exchequer official. His grandson, another Edward, developed the property in the 1680s by utilising the eminently complementary talents of paviour Thomas Green, plasterer Richard Hopkins and brickmaker Richard Tyler – hence Green's Court, Hopkins Street and Tyler's Court on the site of the former Close.

As Sir John Summerson in his *Georgian London* has observed:

'Almost all these men... were 'amateurs' so far as the building industry was concerned; courtiers, soldiers, officials, their only inducement to build was a sense of financial adventure: a belief – not always well-grounded – that to build was as easy a way as any to get rich. It should be added that in most cases they were men whose position enabled them to get by the restrictions on building still nominally in force.'

But there were other kinds of amateurs.

Bridle Lane suggests a leafy by-way, and, indeed, as a thoroughfare it is much older than the surrounding streets; but the name immortalises local carpenter Abraham Bridle, who built houses in Gelding Close, backing onto the Lane, in the 1680s.

Whitcomb Street is the memorial to William of that name, who switched from brewing to building on the strength of leases from Oxenden and Panton. Soho-born Thomas Richmond made a similar career shift from wax-chandler to carpenter and moved on to

12. *Rupert Court in the 1920s. This alleyway and Rupert Street derived their name from Prince Rupert, Royalist hero of the civil wars of the 17th century.*

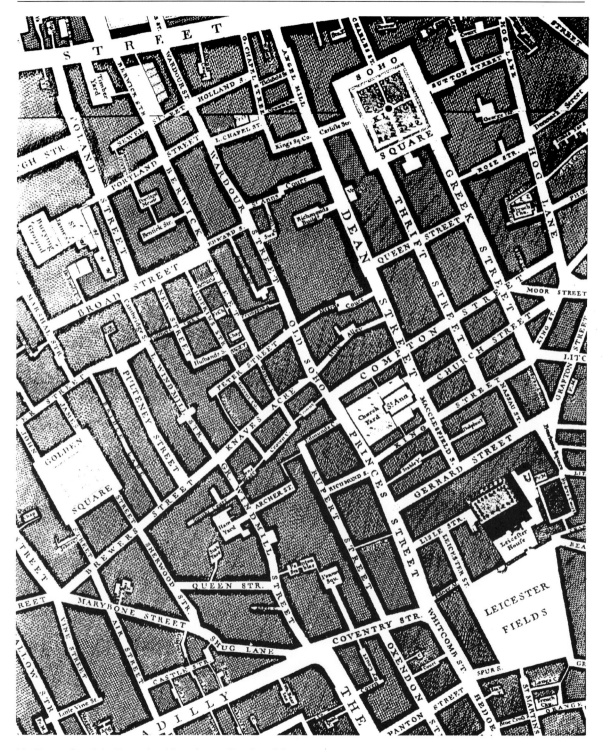

13. *Extract from John Rocque's celebrated map of London of the 1740s. Hog Lane, top right, later called Crown Street, is on the line of the 19th century Charing Cross Road*

build the cul-de-sac known as Richmond Buildings and Richmond Mews.

By far the most ambitious of the humbler sort was bricklayer Richard Frith, a rival to Barbon himself as far as Soho went. Success in erecting a few houses in St James's inspired him to develop the nineteen-acre Soho Field in 1677. Alas, shortly after laying out Soho Square, Frith Street and the adjacent streets, he was squeezed mercilessly on the loans he had taken out to buy building materials and his involvement in the building of Monmouth House sealed his fate, for he and a partner in that particular venture were described as 'very great loosers by the misfortune of the said Duke.' When Frith died, in 1695, he was still in debt.

Meard Street, hailed by Pevsner as 'the most rewarding of all Soho streets', was erected in two phases between 1722 and 1732, by carpenter John Meard, who was also responsible for the long-delayed spire of the parish church.

SHORING UP AND FILLING IN

Although Soho was largely built up in the half century after the Great Fire of London, further development and redevelopment continued intermittently, not least because many of the hastily-built dwellings of the 1680s had to be completely reconstructed when their leases expired forty or fifty years later.

Marshall Street was not begun until the 1720s. The site had the distinctly unattractive but all too accurate name of Pesthouse Close, having been the location of a hospice and burial-pit provided by the Earl of Craven during the Great Plague of 1665 and left in trust at his death for the same purpose should a similar outbreak occur. None did for more than half a century and so Craven's heirs, only too well aware of the value of the site, petitioned Parliament to allow them to substitute a more isolated plot out at Paddington (now Craven Hill) to fulfil the terms of the trust. The Soho property was accordingly developed as a street named for the Craven family seat, Hampstead Marshall in Berkshire.

William III's crony, Hans Bentinck, Earl of Portland, acquired many plots of land through royal favour, among them one on the west side of Wardour

14. *Lisle Street in 1910.*

Street. Houses in what is now Livonia Street once bore a tablet proclaiming it as Bentinck Street and the date 1736. Livonia Street was renamed in 1894. Its name refers to a Baltic province once ruled by Poland, although the street does not actually connect with nearby Poland Street. While Portland Mews celebrates the family connection, another Portland plot was rebuilt in the same decade by Lady Elizabeth Noel, widow of Bentinck's son, the Marquess of Titchfield – hence Noel Street. Fareham Street was originally Titchfield Street but was later renamed after the Hampshire village near Titchfield to distinguish it from the other Titchfield Street, lying to the north, which belonged to the same family.

Lisle Street was laid out in 1791, soon after the demolition of Leicester House, Lisle being the family name of the holders of the Leicester title. Nearby Bear Street may echo the bear and ragged staff which figures in their armorial crest.

Ingestre Place takes its name from Ingestre Buildings, erected in 1853, nominally for the Metropolitan Association for Improving the Dwellings of the Industrious Classes but actually at the initiative of Charles Chetwynd, Viscount Ingestre.

Grandees and Great Houses

A PRIVILEGED QUARTER

Soho's initial character is shown by the eminence of its residents in the 1690s, when there were between sixty and eighty titled inhabitants.

That compulsive conspirator Henry, Viscount Bolingbroke (1678-1751) lived at 21 Golden Square while he was Secretary of War from 1704 to 1708. His next door neighbour was the future Duke of Chandos (which accounts for the later presence in the square of a statue of George II, originally made for the Chandos estate at Canons, Middlesex). Bolingbroke's other neighbours included Barbara Villiers, Duchess of Cleveland, a former mistress of the late Charles II, a bishop, four other peers or future peers and six army officers. The same square, between 1724 and 1788, housed the embassies of Bavaria, Brunswick, Russia, Genoa and, most notably, Portugal, represented by one of its greatest statesmen, the future Marquis de Pombal (1699-1782).

Soho Square had a similar diplomatic community, being home at various times to the envoys of Venice,

15. Henry St John, Viscount Bolingbroke, from the painting by Hyacinth Rigand.

16. Soho Square 1754, by Sutton Nicholls.

Hamstead   Highgate

SOHOE OR KINGS SQUARE

Tiborn Road

Suttons Street

17. *Livonia Street in the 1920s, by Alan Stapleton. Previously called Bentinck Street after one of the Soho grandees, Hans Bentinck, Earl of Portland (see p21).*

18. *Leicester House, Leicester Square.*

Spain, France, Russia and Sweden. Its residents also included no less than three Speakers of the House of Commons, Sir Thomas Littleton (1698-1700), Sir Richard Onslow (1708-10), and one of the most celebrated parliamentarians of the century, Sir Arthur Onslow (1728-1761), whose famous squint made 'catching the Speaker's eye' even more problematic than usual.

Of Great Marlborough Street in 1714 it was written that 'it surpasses anything that is called a street in the magnificence of its buildings and gardens and is inhabited by all prime quality.' Strype, writing about five years later, described Denman Street (then Queen Street) as 'a pretty, neat, clean and quiet Street, with good Houses, well inhabited.'

By the end of the eighteenth century, however, the overall tone of the area had clearly declined. Writing in 1832 the novelist Fanny Burney remembered Poland Street in the 1760s when her neighbours had included a Duke, several other titled persons and, most memorably, a visiting Cherokee chief, and as an address it was not 'as it is now, a sort of street that, like the rest of the neighbourhood, appears to be left in the lurch.'

Further evidence of decline is provided not only by the decay or demolition of great houses and the conversion of properties to commercial use but also by the records of ratepayers. In 1733 twenty-seven Members of Parliament lived in Soho but by 1762 their number had fallen to twelve and by 1793 to four. A list survives from 1791 of subscribers to the evening

patrol, which kept the riffraff off the streets until the regular night watchmen took over. None of the subscribers claimed aristocratic rank, although there were still seven titled ratepayers in the parish of St Anne's. Of those styling themselves 'Esquire', Lisle, King and Gerrard Streets each had one, Frith Street two and Dean Street two plus a 'Captain'. Soho Square alone preserved some exclusivity, with no less than seven 'Esquires', a 'Doctor' and a 'Reverend'. Distinguished residents of the succeeding generation included Sir Joseph Banks, connoisseur and collector Richard Payne Knight, the eminent surgeon Sir Charles Bell and the editor of *The Times*, Thomas Barnes.

LEICESTER HOUSE

Soho's first palatial residence was built by Robert Sidney, second Earl of Leicester, in the 1630s on the northern side of what is now Leicester Square. For a generation it was one of the largest houses in London and had at least thirty rooms, although the builder claimed ingenuously that it was but a 'little House; which was not built for a Levie, but only for a private Family.' Charles I's loyal but unpopular minister, the Earl of Strafford, convalesced there in the summer of 1640. The allegedly healthy situation of the house did little, however, for Charles II's aunt, Elizabeth, Queen of Bohemia, who died there after a week's residence in 1662. Lord Leicester recorded ungraciously that 'It

19. George II

seemes the Fates did not think fit that I should have the Honor, which indeed I never much desyred, to be the Landlord of a Queene'. From 1668 to 1670, however, Lord Leicester was landlord·to the French ambassador.

Diarist John Evelyn dined at Leicester House in 1672 and watched a fire-eater as part of the evening's diversions. From 1677 until his death in 1698 the house was occupied by the third Earl who regularly entertained Dryden and the playwright Wycherley to dinner. The great commander, Prince Eugene of Savoy, Marlborough's comrade-in-arms, lodged there during an abortive diplomatic mission in 1712; the government treated him uncivilly but the mob adored him.

In 1717 the Prince of Wales, the future George II, moved in after being evicted by his father from St James's Palace following a quarrel over the baptism of his son. Here he kept a counter-court for the next decade and was proclaimed monarch outside the gates in 1727. Fifteen years later his son, Frederick, maintained family tradition and annoyed his father by entertaining opposition politicians here. Foolish, feckless Frederick, however, did not succeed to the throne, dying at Leicester House in 1751 after a cricketing accident when the ball hit him in the throat.

In 1774 Leicester House was taken over by a Lancashire naturalist, Ashton Lever, who used it as a museum for his immense collection of fossils, shells, fish, insects and other specimens. Lever, an archery enthu-

siast, was also responsible for forming the Toxopholite Society, which held its initial meeting at Leicester House during his tenancy. The house was demolished in 1791 and its site is now covered by Leicester Place, Lisle Street and the Empire Cinema.

SAVILE HOUSE

Next door to Leicester House stood Savile House, initially known as Ailesbury House after the Jacobite Lord Ailesbury, its intermittent tenant from 1686 to 1698. (He spent most of 1691 hiding at 19 Soho Square and in 1696 was incarcerated in the Tower of London for a year.)

During the future George II's tenancy of Leicester House (1717-27) the two buildings were both occupied by the Prince of Wales and his family and joined by a covered wooden walkway. In 1729 it was renamed Savile House after its new owner, gouty Sir George Savile of Golden Square, but again during the tenancy of Frederick Prince of Wales at Leicester House (1742-51) it formed part of the joint household and was refurbished by the Office of Works, who brought in 'Serjeant-Painter' William Hogarth to work on the decorations.

In 1780 Savile House was looted during the anti-Catholic Gordon Riots because Sir George Savile (the Younger) had been responsible for introducing a Catholic Relief Act into Parliament and his home was therefore singled out by the mob for special attention.

On the night of 5th June 'a large mob of riotous persons... gutted it of best part of the furniture, which they piled up in the street, and set fire to.' They returned on the morning of the 7th 'intoxicated with the wines and spiritous liquors they had plundered' and attacked 'the shell'.

From 1786 until 1805 the plundered residence housed a carpet factory, but following the burning of the King's Theatre in the Haymarket in 1789 plans were drawn up to build a grand opera house on the site of Savile House and designs were submitted by Sir John Soane. The project proved abortive and in 1806 Savile House was remodelled to accommodate both a carpet factory and a permanent gallery in which the embroiderer Mary Linwood (1755-1845) could exhibit her celebrated collection of copies of famous paintings by Gainsborough, Reynolds, Morland and various Italian masters. Subsequent sub-letting of parts of the premises enabled it to house a wondrous variety of entertainments, including 'The Astronomical Panorama', 'Miller's Mechanical and Beautiful Picturesque Representations', 'Sampson's Mechanical and Picturesque Theatre of Arts', the 'Saville Palace Wine, Concert and Exhibition Rooms'

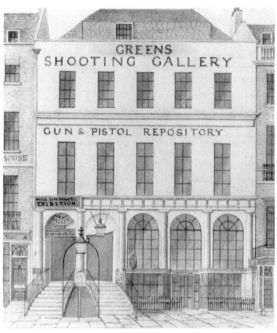

21. Savile House while occupied by Green's Shooting Gallery in c.1840.

20. Exhibition of Miss Linwood's embroidery at Savile House.

LINWOOD GALLERY,
LEICESTER SQUARE.

GRAND MOVING PANORAMA
OF THE

ARCTIC REGIONS

The most interesting Painting now Exhibiting,
Illustrating the

SEARCH FOR SIR JOHN FRANKLIN

In that far Distant and Mysterious Region, for the discovery of whom, a
GOVERNMENT

REWARD OF £20,000

Is now offered to rescue these Adventurers, and long missing Mariners
from their Ice-bound Prison, also the thrilling and perilous Voyages of the
Veteran Sir J. Ross, his daring adventures with the Esquimaux Natives,
their extraordinary Manners and Customs, placing before the Public for
the first time, the Sublime Scenery, and wondrous Phenomena of the Polar
world from Drawings taken on the spot.

Splendid Moving DIAPHARAMA of the
GREAT EARTHQUAKE of LISBON
The OVERFLOWING OF THE TAGUS and Destruction of the
Ill-fated City, with Novel Effect. Concluding with
MISS OSBORN'S NEW ENTERTAINMENT.

EVERY AFTERNOON AT 3, EVENING AT 8,

Admission, 1s.   Reserved Seats, 2s.
SCHOOLS AND CHILDREN HALF-PRICE.
J. W. PEEL's Steam Machine, 74, New Cut, Lambeth

*22. A Panorama staged at Savile House depicting the search
for Sir John Franklin, lost on his mission to find a north-west
passage in north America.*

and a shooting gallery where Edward Oxford prac-
tised before attempting to assassinate Queen Victoria
in 1840. After Mrs Linwood's death her gallery became a theatre, the Walhalla and then a dance-hall,
'Salle Valentino', with an alleged capacity for up to
two thousand devotees of 'the fashionable Quadrille,
the graceful Polka, or the exciting Galop'. By 1852 the
same premises had become a music hall while other
parts of the building were used for exhibitions of
fencing, wrestling, fortune-telling, conjuring and ventriloquism, and in yet other portions could be found
a wine-vault, a coffee-house, gunsmith's, billiard-
room and a maker of invalid chairs. In 1865 a work-
man searched through the basement, looking for a
gas-leak with a lighted candle. The resulting inferno
was watched with interest by the future Edward VII,
who borrowed a fireman's helmet and 'inspected the
conflagration from different points of view.'

Mons. **ROBIN;**
Lately arrived in this Country from the Continent, begs respectfully to inform
Inhabitants of LONDON, that he intends for a stated Period, to EXHIBIT
MATCHLESS COLLECTION of WAX FIGURES, Some of which are FAMIL.
to this COUNTRY, in the UPPER ROOM, at

SAVILLE HOUSE,
Leicester Square,

Open from TEN in the MORNING until FOUR in the AFTERNOON, and from
SIX till TEN in the EVENING.

Admission, Sixpence Each
Children and Servants, Half-price.

A Correct Representation of a

MILITARY EXECUTION,
Of a DESERTER, in the Reign of that great Warrior, NAPOLEON BUONAPARTE.

Mary, Queen of Scots,
Escaping from LOCHLEVEN CASTLE; with her Attendants in a Real Boat, New Scenery,
Dresses, &c. descriptive of the Spot from whence she escaped.

The GRECIAN Daughter,
Visiting her Father in Prison, and giving him Nourishment from her Breast.

An Entirely New ANATOMICAL FIGURE.
A Correct Likeness of Sir Walter Scot.
The beautiful MARINE SPECTACLE, the

SHIPWRECKED SAILOR.
A much admired Group of a NURSE and her CHILDREN.
A striking Likeness of EARL GREY and his Daughter, as large as Life.

Two Beautiful Scripture Pieces
Twelve Figures placed in Two Walnut Shell   of our Saviour, in the Manger at
Bethlehem; and the Offerings of the Wise   being the only Two Groups in
the World in s

An EXACT LIKENESS of Mr. GEE, the   ...or, who was confined by EDWARDS.

The AUTOMATON, or Speaking Figure.
AN EXACT REPRESENTATION OF WILLIAM CORDER;
Also the Figures of Maria Martin and her Child, beautifully executed.
In the Collection will be seen that Phenomenon of Nature lately born, a CHILD with Two Heads.
JONATHAN MARTIN, who set Fire to YORK MINSTER.
Also Striking Likenesses of the following Characters,

Bishop, Williams, and Eliza Ross,
In the same clothes they were executed in.
BURK, HARE, AND WILLIAM SHAW, WITH NUMEROUS OTHERS.
JANE SHORE and the BAKER.
The Wonderful MANIAC of Woodseats, Norton, Derbyshire; who was discovered, having remained
in the position he was found in upwards of FOURTEEN YEARS.
The Celebrated Mary Ann Pearce, better known as Lady Barrymore.
In this Exhibition will be seen, a Large

Boa Constrictor

*23. An exhibition of wax figures at Savile House, depicting
numerous events, such as a military execution, the escape of
Mary, Queen of Scots, as well as various murderers.*

24. *The remains of Savile House, depicted in 1871 following the fire of 1865.*

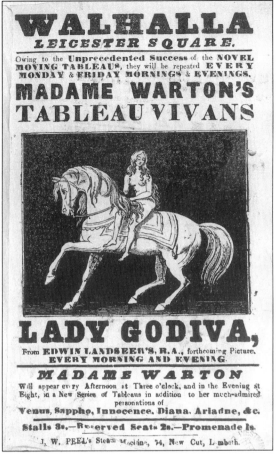

25. Savile House reduced to miscellaneous entertainments, contained the Walhalla in the 1840s which, though begun as a theatre, contained such entertainments as this tableau depicting the legend of Lady Godiva.

The site of Savile House was eventually redeveloped to house the Royal London Panorama, which opened in 1881 to display fifteen thousand square feet of canvas depicting the Charge of the Light Brigade. It opened again in 1884 as the Empire Theatre and again in 1887 as the Empire Palace of Varieties, in which incarnation it finally enjoyed a huge success, somehow managing to combine being a rendezvous for prostitutes and their customers and a reputation for first-class ballet under the inspiration of Adeline Genee. In 1926 the Astaires gave it a brilliant send-off with *Lady, Be Good!*, a highly appropriate title in view of its past. It was converted to a cinema in 1927/8 and sub-divided into a cinema and dance-hall in 1961/3.

MONMOUTH HOUSE

Around 1682 James Scott, Duke of Monmouth (1649-85) and bastard son of Charles II, began to build himself a fine mansion on the south side of Soho (then King's) Square. Although in occupation before it was completed he did not enjoy it long. In 1685, following the death of his royal father, Monmouth attempted to seize the throne with the backing of the credulous but ill-armed peasantry of the West Country; allegedly adopting 'Soho' as their war-cry they were summarily crushed at Sedgemoor, the last battle fought on English soil.

The popular and handsome Monmouth was butchered to death at Tower Hill by a singularly inept executioner who took five strokes to sever his head and then needed a knife to finish the job. Over three hundred of Monmouth's wretched supporters were executed and many more transported across the Atlantic to servitude.

Despite Monmouth's downfall, an interest in the Soho residence was transferred to his wife, but the house was still uncompleted and both this and the ownership became the subject of legal proceedings so complex and protracted that it was virtually uninhabited for thirty years. Meanwhile, between 1689 and 1694, a converted back-room served as a place of worship for recently-arrived Huguenots and was known as *L'Eglise du Quarre*.

In 1717 Monmouth House was finally sold to Sir James Bateman, Lord Mayor of London, who remodelled the front, possibly to the designs of his relative and friend, the architect Thomas Archer, and after a number of distinguished residents, the house was finally condemned to demolition in 1773. The sculp-

26. The Duke of Monmouth.

27. *Monmouth House on the south side of Soho Square. From an engraving for J.T. Smith's* Antiquities of London, *1791.*

tor Joseph Nollekens visited while this was being done, accompanied by his friend and biographer, J.T.Smith, later Keeper of Prints at the British Museum. Even half-ruined Monmouth House was evidently still impressive, with a massive iron gate, mounted on stone piers, and beyond that a spacious courtyard for carriages. The ground floor had eight rooms, with carved and gilded panelling and ornamental plaster ceilings – 'The principal room on the first floor was lined with blue satin, which was superbly decorated with pheasants and other birds in gold.' What the upper floors were originally like could not be recorded as the workmen had already wrecked them.

On the site of Monmouth House were erected two substantial houses, Nos. 28 and 29 Soho Square, and behind them a double row of very modest dwellings – Bateman's Buildings. The first occupant of No. 28 was the manager of the Haymarket Theatre, George Colman, who was followed by Sir Hugh Inglis MP, a director of the East India Company and later by the Radical MP, Joseph Hume. From 1834 to 1860 it served as the recruiting office for the forces of the East India Company, and afterwards as a parsonage house for the Rector of St. Anne's. No. 29 was occupied by the actor Charles Kemble in 1822-5 and demolished in 1875 to make way for extensions to The Hospital for Women

28. St Anne's Rectory in Soho Square.

FAUCONBERG HOUSE

Fauconberg House, in the north-east corner of Soho Square, (now remembered by Falconberg Mews off Sutton Row), was the home from 1683 to 1700 of Thomas Belasyse, first Earl of Fauconberg and from 1753 to 1761 of Speaker Arthur Onslow. A later owner, John Grant, commissioned Robert Adam to carry out improvements for him, notably a radical remodelling of the front, and after Grant's death the house became Wright's Hotel and Coffee House, then the premises of a firm of musical instrument-makers (1810-57) and finally, in 1858, a bottling and labelling plant for Messrs Crosse and Blackwell. They demolished it in 1924 to make way for new offices. The warehouse at the rear of their premises (built after the formation of Charing Cross Road in the 1880s) was later converted to make the Astoria Cinema and Dance Salon.

CARLISLE HOUSE AND CARLISLE HOUSE

Carlisle House number one was at the junction of Sutton Row and Soho Square, where St. Patrick's Roman Catholic Church now stands. It was built around 1685 for the second Earl of Carlisle and remained in the hands of the Howard family until 1753 when the lease was sold to the upholsterers Bradshaw and Saunders, who used the outbuildings as workshops but let the house to the ambassador of the King of Naples (1754-8). But it was during the tenancy of Mrs Cornelys (see p104), from 1760, that the house acquired its London fame. It continued as a place of entertainment after her downfall but no subsequent proprietor had her flair and the house was demolished in 1791 to make way for two modest dwellings, one of which survives as the presbytery of St Patrick's Church.

The second Carlisle House stood virtually opposite, at the far western end of Carlisle Street. Built between 1685 and 1687, it passed through the hands of a number of titled tenants until it was occupied by the Countess of Carlisle, estranged wife of the third Earl, who lived there for nearly thirty years until her death in 1752. In 1763 or 1764 the house was bought by Domenico Angelo Malevolti Tremamondo, better known as Domenico Angelo. He had arrived in England a decade before, soon gained a brilliant reputation as a riding- and fencing-master and was appointed in those capacities to tutor the Prince of Wales, the future George III. Carlisle House gave Angelo the space to cash in on his fame and he built a riding-school in the back garden and took in boarders at 100 guineas a year. He also entertained lavishly at what soon became the most fashionable school of arms and manners in all of London. His guests are known to have included Garrick and the painters Reynolds and Stubbs.

After Angelo left in the 1780s Carlisle House was sub-divided. Many of its tenants were minor artists, picture-restorers and woodcarvers, and a Freemasons' lodge met in the former ballroom. In 1860 it became a boarding-house for 'Clerical, Medical and Law Students', then Whittaker's Private Hotel and, from 1873 to 1936, a warehouse for antique furniture. It was then occupied by the British Board of Film Censors until it was destroyed by enemy bombing on 11th May 1941.

29. *(Top) Part of Carlisle House, Soho Square after its conversion into a Roman Catholic chapel; undated drawing by Howard Penton.*

30. *(Left) The 'School of Eloquence' established briefly at Carlisle House, Soho Square, in 1780 after the departure of Mrs Cornelys.*

31. Carlisle House at the end of Carlisle Street; watercolour by J.P. Emslie.

THE BECKFORDS

No. 22 Soho Square was the home from 1751 until his death of Alderman William Beckford, Lord Mayor of London in 1762 and 1769. Heir to a huge Jamaica fortune, he vigorously defended the cause of the mercurial John Wilkes (1727-97), even so far as an impromptu lecture to an astonished George III on the fundamentals of the British constitution. Beckford's standing in the City for this piece of lèse-majesté can be judged by the fact that he is the only Lord Mayor to have been honoured with a statue in Guildhall, erected barely two years after his death.

Alderman Beckford's son, also William Beckford (1759-1844) was born in the house at Soho Square and while living there received music lessons from the young Mozart. He moved out, still a child, after the death of his father. Later he built a hugely expensive Gothic folly, Fonthill Abbey, where he lived as a recluse, surrounded by books and pictures, until his extravagance obliged him to sell it. He is now chiefly remembered as the author of *Vathek, an Arabian Tale*, composed in French and published in English in 1782. A bizarre oriental fantasy, full of sultans, sin, sorcery

and sacrifices, it was condemned by Hazlitt for the 'diabolical levity of its contempt for mankind', but enjoyed great success.

Five houses away from 22 Soho Square, on the corner of the Square and Greek Street, was the home of Richard Beckford, brother of the older William and uncle of the younger. The original houses on that site were demolished in 1743 and replaced by a large mansion of three storeys, plus basement and garret, built by Joseph Pearce but leased to Beckford, an East India merchant. The surviving plaster ceilings and carved woodwork still bear eloquent testimony to his wealth and taste and are praised by Ann Saunders as 'perhaps the most dramatic example in London of mid-eighteenth century Rococo decoration.' Beckford died in France and, after passing through the hands of a succession of owners who made few significant alterations, the house was sold in 1861 to a charity, established as the House of St. Barnabas-in-Soho in 1846, to relieve London's destitute and homeless – Barnabas being 'the son of consolation'.

The charity's supporters included future Prime Minister William Gladstone and F.D. Maurice, the

founder of Christian Socialism. A chapel, by Joseph Clarke, was added behind the house and its exterior can be seen from Manette Street, which also affords a glimpse of the courtyard and shade tree mentioned in Chapter VI of *A Tale of Two Cities*.

32. (Left) A fanciful depiction of the statue of William Beckford, Lord Mayor of London, in the Guildhall.

33. (Below) The St Barnabas House of Charity at the corner of Soho Square and Greek Street in 1938, from a drawing by Pitts. Note the two-way traffic around the square.

The Newcomers

The first foreigners to settle in any numbers in Soho were Greeks. Between 1677 and 1680 a chapel was built in Hog Lane (now part of Charing Cross Road) under the auspices of Joseph Georgirenes, Archbishop of Samos and with the assistance of Henry Compton, Bishop of London. It was intended as a place of worship for Greeks fleeing from an Ottoman offensive against their homeland. Unfortunately 'legal, financial and personal difficulties', as the *Survey of London* opaquely puts it, beset the project and soon after its completion the Archbishop 'relinquished it in an unhappy atmosphere of suspicion and misunderstanding.' It was not, however, to stay untenanted for long.

34. The inscribed tablet formerly in the Greek Church, Crown Street, and now in the cathedral of Aghia Sophia, Bayswater.

35. The trade card of goldsmith Peter De la Fontaine of Litchfield Street, attributed to William Hogarth.

THE HUGUENOTS

In 1661 Louis XIV of France began actively discriminating against his Protestant subjects (known as Huguenots, a corruption of the German *Eidgenossen*, meaning 'confederates'). For over a century England had given a home to religious refugees – a word the Huguenots themselves introduced to the English language. The tympanum over the entrance to the French Protestant church in Soho Square depicts Edward VI extending a welcome to a distinctly querulous-looking band of arrivals. In July 1681, therefore, Charles II offered 'all such afflicted Protestants' his royal protection and ordered a national collection for their relief and the following year those of the the the newly-arrived Huguenots who settled in Soho took over the vacated Greek chapel in Hog Lane.

In 1685 Louis XIV revoked outright the Edict of Nantes by which, in 1597, his predecessor, Henri IV, had promised toleration for the Huguenots. The trickle of refugees became a flood as 40,000 left their birth-place to cross the Channel. About a third settled in London, notably in Spitalfields, Wandsworth and Soho, all areas outside the boundaries of the City of London and therefore beyond the jurisdiction of City Livery Companies to regulate their trades. The newcomers were industrious, skilled and thrifty people, bringing to their new home not only expertise as silk-weavers, clock-makers, engravers and silver-smiths, but also culinary inventiveness. Oxtail soup, that most English of dishes, was a Huguenot innovation, the English having previously discarded that portion of the animal as useless. The saveloy was another delicacy much favoured by Huguenots – the father of the Soho engraver Matthew Liart is recorded as being a maker of 'survelois'.

By 1692 Soho's Huguenots could attend not only the Hog Lane chapel but had the choice of another in Glasshouse Street, La Patente in Berwick Street, Le Tabernacle in Milk Alley (now Bourchier Street) and Le Quarre in the back of Monmouth House, Soho Square.

In 1711 the vestry of St Anne's, Soho reckoned the population of the parish at 8,133, of whom some forty percent were estimated to be French, the vast majority reckoned as lodgers, rather than householders. Strype in 1720 described the area as having an 'Abundance of French people, many whereof are voluntary Exiles for their Religion... following honest Trades; and some Gentry of the same Nation'; but there is a certain condescension in his dismissal of Old Compton Street as being' of no great Account for its inhabitants which are chiefly French.' By 1739 William Maitland was striking a note of surprise, rather than disdain – 'it is an easy Matter for a Stranger to imagine himself in France.'

Although their numbers included dancing-masters, musicians and wine-merchants, most Soho Hu-

36. 'Noon' by William Hogarth, 1738. It depicts the decorous Huguenots, emerging from their church in Crown Street (formerly the Greek church), in contrast to the more dissolute indigenous population.

37. *Foubert's Place, off Regent Street, in the 1920s. A reminder of the nearby Foubert Riding Academy of the 18th century (see page 39)*

guenots were craftsmen, either silversmiths, silk-weavers, wood-carvers and gunsmiths working to the orders of the wealthy inhabitants of nearby St James's, or designers, engravers and printers, supplying their services to other businesses. James Debaufre, a watchmaker, lived in Church Street (now Romilly Street); gun-makers Pierre Gruche and Jacques Gorgo lived in Compton Street and Grafton Street respectively; James Giles, a china painter, lived in Berwick Street, as did Joseph Duffour, 'Carver and Gilder' and self-proclaimed pioneer manufacturer of papier-mâché. His customers included Frederick, Prince of Wales, for whom he provided gilded picture-frames.

A significant number of Soho Huguenots, however, achieved social eminence or wealth, or both.

One of the earliest was Abraham Meure, who lived in Greek Street from 1691 to 1714 and ran an academy which took in both French and English pupils. It was an elite establishment, offering a curriculum of Latin, French, drawing, dancing and fencing. Another tutor to the aristocracy was M. Jouneau, the minister of the Huguenot church in Berwick Street, who taught the celebrated wit and dilettante, Lord Chesterfield. (Chesterfield also had a Huguenot cook, tailor and doctor.)

Physician Jean Misaubin (1673-1734) was also liv-

38. Sir Samuel Romilly.

ing in Berwick Street when, in 1709, he married Marthe Angibaud, whose father later became Master of the Society of Apothecaries. Despite his father-in-law's settlement of £400 Misaubin's marriage does not appear to have been a great success, for at his death he left his considerable fortune to his son, while his wife got merely his best French Bible and a shilling.

Portraitist and art-dealer Philip Mercier (1689-1760), who lived at 40 Leicester Square, was appointed Principal Painter and Library Keeper to Frederick, Prince of Wales in 1729. Mercier painted many studies in the style of Watteau, whom he may have entertained on his visit to London in 1719-20, and he also painted the portrait of the Huguenot Lieutenant General De Jean, who served in the Grenadiers, commanded a volunteer militia of London Swiss and became Director of the French Hospital, the leading Huguenot charity. After Mercier's death his widow, Dorothy, opened a shop in Little Windmill Street where she sold imported prints, artists' supplies, fans and 'Flower Pieces in Water Colours Painted by herself from life.'

Nicholas Sprimont, a trained silversmith, lived in Old Compton Street from 1742 to 1770. He was a collaborator of the goldsmith Paul Crespin and a close friend of the eminent sculptor Roubiliac. As the director of the Chelsea porcelain factory Sprimont struggled to make it a worthy rival to Sèvres. His neighbour Matthew Liart, who lived in the same street for most of his life (c1736-c1782), was a well-known engraver. Liart's fellow-engraver Philip Audinet (1766-1837) was actually born in Soho and educated there by his uncle, the Rev. Samuel Audinet.

Matthew Maty (1718-1776), lived in Frith Street from 1752 to 1756, when he was working as an under-librarian at the newly-established British Museum. He was also single-handedly producing a monthly *Journal Britannique*, which was intended to acquaint French readers with English literature. A generous benefactor of the Museum, Maty, a Fellow of the Royal Society, was also a regular patron of Slaughter's Coffee House in St Martin's Lane. This was a favoured resort of French-speaking intellectuals and Dr Johnson came there to improve his grasp of the language. When Maty had the temerity to criticise his famous *Dictionary* Johnson called him 'a little black dog' and threatened to throw him in the Thames. Johnson was on much better terms with another distinguished Huguenot, the MP Anthony Chamier (1725-80) who was a founder-member of the Club (see p42). Chamier's portrait was painted by Reynolds on no less than three occasions.

The most eminent Soho Huguenot of them all was Sir Samuel Romilly (1757-1818). The son of a Frith Street jeweller, he rose far beyond his humble origins to become a leading law-reformer and, as Solicitor

39. *Livery stables 1801, formerly the home of Foubert's Riding Academy, then in Swallow Street.*

General, abolished the death penalty for mugging, while opposing slavery and supporting Catholic emancipation. Romilly was also influential in promoting the career of his nephew, the physician and polymath Peter Mark Roget (1779-1869). Born in Broadwick Street, Roget not only had a successful medical practice but also served as Secretary of the Royal Society and helped to found the University of London. He is chiefly remembered for the *Thesaurus* which was the product of his retirement years, and first published in 1852 – it went through twenty-eight editions even before his death.

By the last quarter of the eighteenth century the Huguenots had been largely assimilated into British society, rather than constituting a separate and distinctive community and by 1800 there were only eight French Protestant churches in all of London, and by 1900 only three and nowadays only one – in Soho Square.

A few of Soho's street-names recall its former character as a French *quartier*, and some are misleading. Sheraton Street was, until 1937, Little Chapel Street, commemorating the chapel known as La Petite Patente, where Huguenots worshiped from 1694 until 1784, after which the building passed first to the Methodists (to 1796), then to Scottish Presbyterians, who rebuilt it in 1824, and finally to Wesleyans (1889),

before it was demolished in 1894. Foubert's Place was originally Major Foubert's Passage, an alley which ran beside the fashionable riding-school run by the Foubert family until 1778. Dufour's Court takes its name from its builder, Paul Dufour, who is possibly the Captain Defour or Defaux who lived at 54 Poland Street from 1705 to 1740.

What appears to derive from a Huguenot name, D'Arblay Street, is however from the married name of Fanny Burney; Bourchier Street, formerly Little Dean Street and, before 1838, Milk Alley, was renamed as a tribute to the Rev. Basil Bourchier (1881-1934), rector of St Anne's.

THE OTHERS

The Italian poet Ugo Foscolo had many followers in finding a haven in Soho. Political refugees from failed revolutions were succeeded by economic migrants and by 1886 they were numerous enough to found the *Societa Italiana Cuochi-Camerieri*, a benefit and social club for Italian workers in the catering trade. It also functioned as an informal labour exchange for new arrivals seeking work. Within ten years the club had four hundred and fifty members and was wealthy enough to buy the lease of 27 Soho Square and employ a paid secretary and steward. Music, cards and bicy-

40. *The Soho Italian Club band.*

cle races round Soho Square appear to have been the favourite pastimes of its members.

Among Soho's German population musicians and makers of musical instruments were especially prominent. J.C. Smith (originally Schmidt) had his son educated at Clare's Academy in Soho Square. Johann Christian Bach (1735-82) and Carl Friedrich Abel, who managed the remarkable feat of numbering both Mrs Cornelys and the ultra-respectable Queen Charlotte among their patrons, shared lodgings together successively in Meard Street, King's Square Court and Queen Street, off Golden Square. They were active, with Handel, in helping to found the (later Royal) Society of Musicians in 1738 as a charitable organisation for the relief of indigent instrumentalists. Their initiative was prompted by the discovery that two orphaned sons of the oboist Kytch had been seen, dressed in tatters, herding livestock down to Haymarket. The nineteenth century brought an influx of German political refugees, notably after the failed revolutions of 1848, as well as humbler migrants who found employment in Soho as craftsmen, garment-workers, waiters, bakers, butchers and publicans.

Flora Tristan, the French radical, noted the existence of a severely impoverished Jewish community in the Newport Market area in the 1840s and there was a synagogue somewhere in Dean Street around the same time. A Western Jewish Girls' Free School was in existence by the 1850s, initially at 21 Dean Street, then at 6 Greek Street. The Jewish presence in Soho was further strengthened by the emigration of Russian and Polish Jews after the pogroms of the 1880s. At the end of that decade a West-Central Jewish Girls' Club was founded by Lady Battersea and Miss Emily Harris. By 1898 it had over two hundred members, of whom about sixty could usually be found at its Dean Street headquarters each evening. Classes were offered in musical drill, French, English, Hebrew, basket-weaving, singing, cooking, laundry and first aid, and new immigrants were given coaching in reading and writing English. Saturday evenings were given over to less serious pursuits – music, dances and a monthly debate, and Sundays meant tea and a lecture, followed by dancing. The supervising ladies came from such areas as Kensington, Bayswater and Maida Vale. The actual members included domestic servants, stationers and makers of wigs and cigars, but the overwhelming number were employed in Soho workshops in various branches of the garment trade, making caps, waistcoats or dresses.

Many Jewish men also found employment as outworkers in the tailoring business, cutting, sewing and pressing for the up-market Savile Row houses on the other side of Regent Street. In 1917 the West End Talmud Torah and Bikkur Holim Synagogue took over the old workhouse in Manette Street, which functioned as a synagogue until 1941. By 1944 the congregation had taken over the former St Anne's National School building at Dean Street and in 1961 this was demolished and replaced by a new building incorporating a youth club and the gallery of the Ben Uri Art Society.

A survey of ethnic minorities in Soho in the 1890s estimated that they totalled 4,295. Of these the largest groups were the Germans (1,070), French (901), Italians (652) and Poles (481). There were also substantial numbers of Swiss (258), Russians (232), Belgians (174), Swedes (127), Austrians (107), Dutch (88) and Americans (81). There were a few Spaniards (29), Hungarians (27) and Danes (26), but scarcely any Turks (9) or Greeks (7). And although there were four each of Portuguese, Rumanians and (undifferentiated) 'Africans', and even two Persians and a solitary Serb – there was not one single Chinese.

The Chinese presence, now so evident around Gerrard Street, is very largely a post-war phenomenon. As recently as 1950 *The Wonderful Story of*

42. A concert at the Soho Jewish Girls' Club.

London could observe that 'Not many Chinese live in Soho, though they run several restaurants there and in that vicinity'. Now the Chinese Chamber of Commerce in Soho houses the largest Chinese-language school in Europe, with 900 pupils enrolled.

41. The Soho Jewish Girls' Club

Salons and Saloons

CONVIVIAL ENCOUNTERS

At 35 St Martin's Street, on the south side of Leicester Square, Westminster Public Library now stands on the site of the former home of Sir Isaac Newton (1642-1727). By the time he came to live there in 1710 he was already in his seventies and though occasionally occupied by his duties as Master of the Royal Mint, he also dozed through the meetings of the Royal Society, over which he continued to preside. Far from the most clubbable of men, Newton's visitors at St Martin's Street nonetheless included the playwright Congreve, the versifying diplomat Matthew Prior, the poet and royal physician John Arbuthnot and Jonathan Swift, who took lodgings round the corner in Leicester Square in 1711, when at the height of his influence as a pamphleteer.

Half a century later the same house was occupied by the distinguished musicologist Dr Charles Burney (1726-1814) and his large family. It was here that his fourth child, Fanny (1752-1840), composed *Evelina, or The History of a Young Lady's Entrance into the World* (1778), an epistolary novel which stunned the literary world. Published anonymously, it remained unacknowledged by the author until she heard Dr Samuel Johnson (1709-84), the leading critic of the age, praising it to her father.

Johnson himself was no stranger to Soho, being a founder-member of 'The Club' established in 1764 at the Turk's Head in Gerrard Street by Sir Joshua Reynolds. It met weekly on Mondays for dinner and conversation, latterly fortnightly while Parliament sat. Attendance was taken seriously, with fines for defaulters. Other members included the playwrights Oliver Goldsmith and Richard Sheridan, the bibliophile, Topham Beauclerk, Johnson's protege, the actor-manager David Garrick and his biographer, James Boswell and the statesman, Edmund Burke, who also lodged at 37 Gerrard Street. During the anti-Catholic Gordon Riots of 1780 the Turk's Head served as the headquarters for the magistrates of Westminster and Middlesex. By the 1790s, 'The Club', by now at Prince's in Sackville Street, had a membership of thirty-five, including the historian Edward Gibbon, the orientalist and philologist Sir William Jones and the scientist Sir Joseph Banks.

Banks, who lived at 32 Soho Square for almost half a century, carried forward this tradition of intellectual brilliance. As a young man he accompanied Captain Cook's circumnavigation of the globe in 1768-71, returning with 3,600 plants, a third of them never before classified. Banks became a founder of the Botanical Gardens at Kew and served as President of the Royal Society from 1778 until the year before his death. It was at his house that the inaugural meeting of the Royal Institution took place in 1799; its main purposes were to promote and diffuse scientific knowl-

43. Sir Isaac Newton.

44. Fanny Burney.

45. *Sir Isaac Newton's house in St Martin's Street, Leicester Square.*

46. *The Turk's Head, Gerrard Street, where the first meetings of the Literary Club met (see p42).*

47. *Sir Joshua Reynolds*

48. *Sir Joseph Banks.*

edge under the well-qualified direction of Sir Humphrey Davy and his assistant Michael Faraday. It was an entirely appropriate tribute to such a distinguished botanist that, after Banks' death, his former home became the regular meeting-place of the Linnaean Society from 1821 to 1857.

But Soho has more typically provided the venue for informal gatherings of artists and writers than for the decorous proceedings of learned societies. In the eighteenth century that easy-going dilettante James 'Athenian' Stuart was the leading light of a group of artists and art-lovers who gathered at the Feathers in Leicester Place and subsequently at the Blue Posts in Dean Street. Stuart, having travelled widely in the Near East, published *The Antiquities of Athens* which, being based on rare first-hand acquaintance, made him an acknowledged expert on the classical world. Following Hogarth's death in 1764 Stuart succeeded him as royal 'Serjeant-Painter' and in 1766 moved into No. 35 Leicester Square, where he decorated his parlour with Hogarth prints.

At the beginning of the present century the Mont Blanc restaurant at 16 Gerrard Street served as the gathering-place for a loose literary network whose

49. A literary party at the home of Sir Joshua Reynolds. Guests from left to right are Boswell, Dr Johnson, Reynolds, David Garrick, Burke, Paoli, Charles Burney, Warton and Goldsmith.

50. John Galsworthy, a regular at the Mont Blanc restaurant in Gerrard Street.

members included the essayists Hilaire Belloc and G. K. Chesterton, the novelists John Galsworthy, Joseph Conrad and Ford Madox Ford, and the poets John Masefield, W.H. Davies and Edward Thomas.

Nearby, at a café at 67 Frith Street, a more diverse group congregated – writer Middleton Murry, editor and translator Edward Marsh, poet-philosopher T.E. Hulme and his friend, sculptor Jacob Epstein, recently arrived from his native New York.

After the Great War T.S. Eliot and his collaborators met at the Commercio in Frith Street to plan the launch of his influential critical journal *Criterion*.

A more formal group came into being in the late 1920s with the establishment of the Detection Club, whose members were all mystery writers. They met in rooms on the first floor of 31 Gerrard Street, one of the very few houses to survive from the late seventeenth century. Members were initiated annually at a banquet, presided over by the Ruler, clad in Chinese robes – a post held by G.K. Chesterton, Dorothy Sayers, Agatha Christie, Julian Symons and H.R.F. Keating. The Rite of Initiation, written by Sayers, was a parody of *The Book of Common Prayer* which required candidates to pledge themselves never to write plots which depended on 'Divine Revelation, Feminine Intuition, Mumbo-Jumbo, Jiggery-Pokery, Coinci-

51. *G.K. Chesterton*

dence or the Act of God', to be moderate in their invocation of 'Gangs, Conspiracies, Death-Rays, Ghosts... Trap-doors, Chinamen... and utterly forswear Mysterious Poisons unknown to Science.' After the Second World War the club acquired the use of a room in Kingly Street through Dorothy Sayers' church connections.

BOHEMIA

By the 1920s Soho had begun to stake its claim to a presence on the night-club scene. The notorious '43' was run at 43 Gerrard Street by the headline-grabbing Mrs Meyrick, who in her colourful *Secrets of the 43 Club* (1933) erroneously invoked Dryden as a guardian spirit of her enterprise – 'I could picture the old poet so clearly, sitting at his desk, with sheets of paper strewn around him...'.

Mrs Meyrick's regular clientele, unsurprisingly, embraced few poets, though it did include Conrad, Epstein and journalist-dramatist J.B. Priestley. These may have been welcome but not perhaps as much as Lancashire millionaire Jimmy White, who turned up one night with six Daimlers full of showgirls and binged £400 on champagne. Just opposite the '43' stood a restaurant run by 'Brilliant' Chang, who supplied more stimulating substances than chop suey to Mrs. Meyrick's patrons. The '43' was first raided by police in 1923 and the following year the proprietress was gaoled for six months in Holloway Prison. Imprisoned again in 1929-30, she battled gamely on. Whatever the '43' cost her personally it did enable her

to marry three of her daughters into the peerage.

The Café de Paris at 3-4 Coventry Street was patronised by kings of Greece, Norway, Spain and Portugal, the Prince of Wales (1894-1972) and Noel Coward (1899-1973); its cabaret starred such names as Marlene Dietrich and Maurice Chevalier and its dance-hostesses included Merle Oberon and Norma Shearer. The decor was based on the Palm Court of the ill-starred luxury liner, *S.S. Lusitania.* The subterranean Café – advertised as 'the safest place to dance in Town' – proved similarly vulnerable to the fortunes of war, receiving a direct hit from a German bomb on 8th March 1941; the eventual death toll was eighty. On the same night a direct hit on the Madrid restaurant in Dean Street killed another seventeen.

The Gargoyle in Meard Street proved more durable. Created by socialite the Hon. David Tennant and actress Hermione Baddeley, it boasted a top-floor ballroom which incorporated the work of Matisse and Lutyens and a clientele which included dancer Fred Astaire, actress Tallulah Bankhead and double-agents Burgess and Maclean. By the 1950s, however, the fashionable, if considerably less elegant, setting for flamboyant dissipation was the Colony Club in Dean Street, presided over by the formidable and foul-mouthed Muriel Belcher. Its regular denizens included the artists Francis Bacon and Lucien Freud and Sixties satirist Peter Cook. Daniel Farson's *Soho in the Fifties* treats it as a focal point of Soho life and chronicles in detail its role in maintaining the alcoholic momentum of its inhabitants.

There were, however, plenty of others to go to – Club des Caves de France ('social club for French speaking people and meeting place for poets, painters, writers and artists'); Club Côte d'Azur, (*'Un coin de Provence a Londres. Aimez vous le Mambo?'*); Club Tahiti ('Gay and colourful'); Little Sweden Club (Swedish smorgasbord, American bar.); Mandrake Club ('Soho's rendezvous of Bohemia'); Miranda's Club ('Ambiance Francaise') – not to mention the Gay Compton Club, Sorrento Club, The Mazurka, Fleur de Lys, Campari, New Panama Club, New Haymarket Club and the apparently high-minded Visual Arts Club whose members were committed to the egalitarian belief 'that the practice of art is the privilege of all and the appreciation of art the common ground of all.'

By the Fifties Soho had become noted for another novelty, described at the time as 'varied, international, stimulating' – the coffee bar, whose function was far more social than nutritional. With the headquarters of Gaggia Espresso coffee machines at 10 Dean Street, Soho's pre-eminence was virtually inevitable. Old Compton Street alone mustered the Prego Bar Restaurant, Act One Scene One ('Real French coffee. Where the film and theatrical celebrities gather'), Heaven and Hell ('Visit the unusual decor of the dive basement') and the Two I's, run by a couple

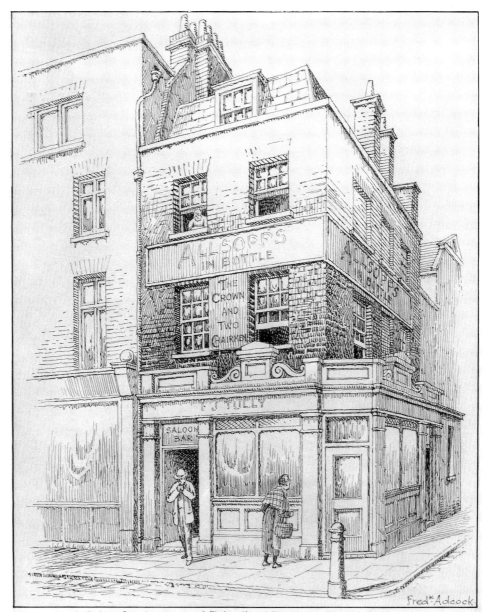

THE CROWN AND TWO CHAIRMEN · DEAN STREET ·

The only inn of this name in London. It was here the sedan chairmen waited when Queen Anne was sitting for her portrait at Sir James Thornhill's house, N°74, still standing on the opposite side of the street. The Crown and Two Chairmen is said to be the house where George Augustus Sala first met Thackeray and heard him sing "The Mahogany Tree".

52. *The Crown and Two Chairmen in Dean Street, by Frederick Adcock.*

53. *The French House in Dean Street, officially known for many years as the York Minster.*

of Australians but named for their landlords, the Irani brothers. In Dean Street Les Enfants Terribles offered 'Music, songs and laughter *à la Française*', while the Moka bar in Frith Street claimed to be 'London's first Espresso coffee bar. Patronised by over fifty nationalities.' In Carlisle Street the Partisan coffee bar was a centre for left-wing discussion and personalities.

If Britain in the 1950s was dreary, dry and dull it certainly wasn't Soho's fault.

PUBS

Soho has more than a dozen public houses which can be traced back to the first half of the eighteenth century. Bateman Street's Dog and Duck (1734) is a reminder of the times when sportsmen could shoot snipe in nearby Leicester Fields. The Charles Norton Centre for senior citizens stands on the site of the Crown (1740) and there was another public house of the same name in Dean Street (1724). In *Nicholas Nickleby* Dickens has Newman Noggs resident at a Crown Inn in Beak Street, where the Sun and Thirteen Cantons is a reminder of Soho's old-established Protestant Swiss community: the Scots House on the corner of Romilly Street was, until 1908, known as the George and Thirteen Cantons. The Coach and Horses in the same street was certainly in existence by 1734; it is now the famed local of *Spectator* columnist and

character, Jeffrey Bernard, and also numbers among its patrons actors Tom Baker, John Hurt and Michael Elphick. Its namesake in Great Marlborough Street dates from 1739. To compound the confusion the Glasshouse Stores in Brewer Street was also known as the Coach and Horses from 1730 until 1875. The late-Victorian St James's Tavern in Great Windmill Street stands on the site of the Catherine Wheel (1733).

A number of Soho pubs can claim more than mere antiquity and a colourful clientele.

The Intrepid Fox is not another echo from the sporting past but a tribute to Charles James Fox (1749-1806), gambler, libertine and Radical candidate for Westminster in the hotly-contested election of 1784. Landlord Sam House, an ardent Foxite, offered free drinks to all who would vote for his hero and the Duchess of Devonshire favoured each supporter with a kiss.

The French House at 49 Dean Street was, for most of its existence, officially called The York Minster, but was universally known as 'the French' after coming under the proprietorship of M. Berlemont in 1914. Its Gallic atmosphere proved irresistible to such self-conscious Bohemians as portraitist Augustus John, playwright Brendan Behan and poet Dylan Thomas. During the Second World War 'the French' became an informal headquarters for the Free French in London, as the nearby 'De Hems' in Macclesfield Street did for Dutch exiles and resisters.

Ladies of Independent Temper

MARY DELANY AND HESTER CHAPONE

Soho has long provided a home for women determined to go their own way – we shall encounter Mrs Cornelys, Elizabeth Price and Peg Woffington in later chapters. Others not so well-known are also worth recording.

In 1721-2 Mrs Mary Delany was living in Manette Street with her elderly, jealous and singularly unpleasant husband, a Cornish squire named Pendarves, who had lost badly in the South Sea Company trading swindle and taken to drink and gambling to forget his sorrows. He soon obliged her by dying, but left her only enough to pay for two rooms and a half-share in a maid. A prolific letter writer and an avid collector of shells and flowers, the Widow Pendarves numbered Swift, Burke, John Wesley and Horace Walpole among her acquaintance. At the age of forty-three she married a friend of Swift's, the Irish divine, Patrick Delany. He was nearly sixty but their marriage lasted for twenty-five years and they lived very comfortably, dividing their time between Ireland, London and Bath. After his death Mrs Delany became a favourite of the royal family and was responsible for introducing Fanny Burney to court – a dubious favour in view of the excruciating tedium Fanny endured there. The definitive collection of painted, paper flowers she made in her old age – the *Flora Delanica* – eventually filled nine hundred and eighty volumes and was praised by Banks, the leading botanist of the age, as 'the only imitations of nature I have seen from which I would venture to describe botanically any plant without the least fear of committing an error'. They are now deposited in the British Museum.

Hester Chapone (1721-1801) was brought up in a house in King's Square Court (now demolished) on the site now occupied by 90 Dean Street. A precocious child, who soon mastered French, Italian and Latin, and was also accomplished in music and sketching. Dr Johnson thought highly enough of her to invite her to contribute to *The Rambler*; the novelist Samuel Richardson, thirty years her senior, also admired her, calling her 'little spit-fire'. She was a prominent member of the 'Bluestocking' circle, which met for conversation only, forswearing the fashionable distractions of cards and alcohol. At Bluestocking gatherings tea, and coffee were permitted – politics, scandal and swearing were not. Half the company was usually female. Johnson was much lionised at their meetings, which were held in the homes of leading members of the group and also in the houses of Sir Joshua Reynolds

54. Samuel Richardson, an admirer of Hester Chapone.

and Mrs Thrale; Boswell, Garrick, Richardson and Horace Walpole were all regular attenders. In her thirties Mrs Chapone published verse tales, and in her fifties, essays. Of these the most important appeared as *Letters on the Improvement of the Mind*. By her sixties she was back in Soho again living briefly in Dean Street. Mrs Chapone's writings went through numerous editions and a complete edition of her works appeared posthumously in 1807.

THE CHEVALIER D'EON

The Chevalier d'Eon spent much of his or her life defying gender. Soldier, spy, diplomat and peerless swordsman, he lived at 38 (now 71) Brewer Street for thirty-three years. Arriving in London in 1762, the Chevalier swiftly won the reputation of an outstandingly loyal and diligent diplomat in an embassy torn by discord – so much so that in 1763, when the ambassador was recalled, he was left as *chargé d'affaires*. Alas, the new ambassador proved to be the Comte de Guerchy, an old adversary of d'Eon. They soon quarrelled and d'Eon became convinced that he was being spied on, then poisoned as a preliminary to abduction. He therefore exchanged his Dover Street lodgings for rooms in the house of a Belgian wine merchant in Brewer Street. Here he virtually barricaded himself in, mining the house with explosives and employing former regimental comrades as additional guards in the event of an assault by French agents. The French government realised that the formerly trusted d'Eon possessed much confidential information that could prove hugely damaging to Anglo-French relations, which were just settling down after the Seven Years War. It was therefore judged more prudent to pension him off in return for reports on the English political scene. D'Eon therefore settled down in Brewer Street in exile, sustained by an excellent supply of in-house wines and a library of 8,000 books.

Living in a district substantially populated by diplomats, politicians, writers, theatricals and other professional gossips, the Chevalier was a popular guest at dinners and receptions but also became the subject of rumour as a result of his plumpish figure, fine features, soft voice and apparent indifference to women. Word that he had actually dressed as a woman while on an espionage mission at the Russian court fuelled the speculation still further. By 1775 the *Morning Post* was declaring that the odds were 7:4 in favour of his being a man and £120,000 was said to have been laid in bets on the question. In 1777 the issue appeared to have been finally settled when d'Eon appeared in public dressed in a gown and sporting a diamond head-dress. On returning to France, d'Eon was presented and accepted as a woman. (Marie-Antoinette added the bill for a new wardrobe to her own already over-extended account.) The French government had evidently decided that this course offered the most practicable way of controlling this embarrassing maverick. D'Eon decided otherwise, returning to England. The revolution of 1789 cut off his income, both from the state and his family properties, and she/he – now permanently dressed as a woman – was forced to scrape a living by playing exhibition chess matches and putting on displays of fencing with the actress Mrs Bateman, who lived at the corner of Carlisle Street and Soho Square. After sustaining a serious accident in a fencing bout at the age of sixty-seven d'Eon lived out enforced retirement on the charity of a kind Frenchwoman and helped out with mending the linen. Dying in 1810 at the age of eighty-one, d'Eon shocked the world yet again. Laying out the corpse revealed unmistakably that 'Madamoiselle' was indeed 'a very man'.

MRS THRALE AND MRS INCHBALD

Hester Lynch Salusbury (1741-1821) of Dean Street also had the last laugh, in her own way. Married, much against her own wishes, to a trying brewer, Henry Thrale, at St Anne's, Soho in 1763, she nevertheless became a supportive wife and generous hostess to the frequently irascible Dr Johnson. When her husband finally died she soon married, to the outrage of Johnson, a personable Italian musician called Piozzi. She was very happy, returning to Soho to live first of all in Great Marlborough Street and later in an hotel

55. *Hester Thrale.*

on Leicester Square which had formerly been Hogarth's house.

Mrs. Elizabeth Inchbald (1753-1821) ran away from home in Bury St. Edmunds at the age of eighteen to join her brother, the actor George Simpson, and succeeded in her ambition to become an actress despite a speech impediment which she never entirely overcame (contemporaries found it charming). Mrs Inchbald knew Sarah Siddons and was a friend of the radical William Godwin – until his marriage to proto-feminist Mary Wollstonecraft. After the death of her ineffectual actor husband, and while she was living in Frith Street, she turned to writing full-time. Much of her dramatic work rested on translations from French or German and its emotionality attracted the sardonic attention of Jane Austen; her play *Lovers' Vows* is the drama chosen for enactment by the Bertrams in *Mansfield Park*.

Elizabeth Inchbald also lived, from 1798 until 1803, in the same hotel as Mrs Piozzi. As a freelance dramatist Mrs Inchbald was exposed to perils akin to those of the casting couch. On one occasion she was virtually assaulted by a potential producer but had the presence of mind to grab his hair with one hand while ringing a bell for assistance with the other. Recounting her narrow escape afterwards she always concluded the anecdote with the observation 'How f - fortunate for me he did NOT W-EAR a W - IG.'

Exiles

A CORSICAN 'KING'

The figure of the exile is almost by definition a tragic one, but Theodore, the would-be King of Corsica, is also tinged with absurdity. Born Theodore Anthony Neuhoff, he spent a footloose youth in Europe before getting mixed up in the Corsican struggle for independence from the rule of mainland Genoa. His timely enterprise in running guns to the rebels brought him, in rapid order, acclamation, coronation and deposition. Fleeing, virtually penniless, to London in 1756 he was soon imprisoned for debt. Deliverance came providentially in the shape of a new Act of Parliament revising the conditions on which debtors could negotiate their release from prison. Suddenly free, but with neither resources nor prospects, Theodore 'took a chair and went to the Portuguese minister, but did not find him at home; not having sixpence to pay, he persuaded the chairman to carry him to a tailor he knew in Soho, whom he prevailed upon to harbour him, but he fell sick the next day, and died in three

more.' A Compton Street oilman was intrigued enough at the thought of paying for a royal funeral to cover the costs of the burial at St Anne's and the connoisseur Horace Walpole paid for a tombstone and composed a fitting epitaph:

> The grave, great teacher, to a level brings
> Heroes and beggars, galley-slaves and kings.
> But Theodore this moral learn'd e'er dead;
> Fate pour'd its lesson on his living head,
> Bestow'd a kingdom, and denied him bread.

FRENCH NOTABLES

It would be surprising, perhaps, if such a vast and dramatic upheaval as the French revolution had not touched cosmopolitan Soho. Foremost in this respect was Swiss-born Jean-Paul Marat (1743-93), who settled in London in the 1770s, establishing a reputation as a society physician and experimental scientist. In 1776 he published a treatise on diseases of the eye from an address in Romilly Street. Returning to France he became an influential newspaper editor and spokes

56. The 'King' of Corsica.

57. The 'King' of Corsica's tombstone, with its inscription composed by Horace Walpole.

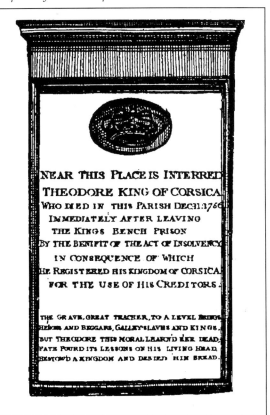

58. Madame de Stael.

59. Ugo Foscolo.

man for the revolutionary cause before meeting a melodramatic end at the hands of Charlotte Corday.

Mme Germaine de Stael (1766-1817) owes her reputation to literature rather than politics, although she was also influential among French emigré circles. As the daughter of Louis XVI's ill-fated finance minister she was, at sixteen, spoken of as a possible bride for the younger Pitt but opted instead for a marriage of convenience to a Swedish diplomat. Her analysis of the writings of Jean-Jacques Rousseau established her critical reputation and brought her in due course the friendship of such leading Romantic writers as Constant, Schlegel and Byron. Her liberalism brought the enmity of Napoleon upon her – and consequent exile, including residence at 20 Argyll Street in 1813-14.

FOSCOLO AND ACCUM

Ugo Foscolo (1778-1827), the 'Italian Lord Byron', having made his name as poet, patriot and paramour, fled to London after the reimposition of Austrian rule over northern Italy. His residence at 11 Soho Square from 1816 to 1818 represented an all too brief period of prosperity. As the acclamation faded he was forced to rely on his pen for a niggardly income. He died, in great poverty, at Turnham Green. In 1871 his body was repatriated with much pomp to Florence for reburial.

The Prussian scientist Friedrich Accum (1769-1839) lived at 33 Old Compton Street from 1803 to 1822. Supporting himself by working as an assistant to Sir Humphry Davy at the Royal Institution, Accum played a leading role in introducing gas-lighting to the streets

of London and undertook pioneering work in the detection and exposure of food adulteration. This latter project brought him into conflict with powerful commercial interests which may have been behind the disgrace which brought about his downfall. Accused of removing colour-plates from books, he was dismissed from his post and eventually hounded out of the country.

ENGELS AND MARX

The failure of the German revolutions of 1848 brought Soho its two most famous exiles, Friedrich Engels (1820-95) and Karl Marx (1818-83). Both men had visited London in 1847 when they had addressed the German Workers' Education Society. Fleeing Germany via Paris in the summer of 1849, Marx settled first in Camberwell, then Chelsea before debt drove him to temporary refuge in the German Hotel (now Manzi's), just off Leicester Square until 'one morning our host refused to serve us our breakfast and we were forced to look for other lodgings.'

From May to December 1850 the Marxes lodged with a Jewish lace dealer at 64 Dean Street and then took two rooms on the top floor of 28 Dean Street, which was to be their home for the next six years. The census of 1851, which recorded Marx as 'Charles Mark, Doctor (Philosophical Author)', reveals that the other inhabitants of the house were an Italian confectioner and a language teacher, from whom the Marxes sub-let. The landlord was another Italian, John Marengo, a cook.

Having secured a ticket for the Reading Room of

60. *Karl Marx*

the British Museum in June 1850, Marx divided his time between studying there and writing in the Dean Street attic. He also served on a relief committee for refugees even more impoverished than he was and took occasional exercise fencing at a 'salon' in Rathbone Place, which was on his route back from Bloomsbury. When the opportunity arose he held court to visiting revolutionaries and even entertained a Prussian police agent, who reported on the exile's squalor with a curious mixture of distaste and compassion:

'Marx lives in one of the worst, therefore one of the cheapest, quarters of London... In the whole apartment there is not one clean and solid piece of furniture. A seller of second-hand goods would be ashamed to give away such a remarkable collection of odds and ends... Everything is dirty and covered with dust, so that to sit down becomes a thoroughly dangerous business.'

Characterising Marx as 'an extremely disorderly, cynical human being' who smoked incessantly, rarely washed and was frequently drunk, the same agent conceded that he was also a warm-hearted father and a willing, if spasmodic, worker:

'Though he is often idle for days on end, he will work day and night with tireless endurance when he has a great deal of work to do. He has no fixed times

61. *No. 28 Dean Street, the home of Karl Marx and his family for six years.*

62. *'A Communist club-room near Leicester Square'; from the* Illustrated London News, *6 January 1872. Upon the rout of Communards in France a great many sought refuge in London. Leicester Square and Soho became their Quartier Général and a club was formed based on a public house in Rupert Street where only those who could prove that they had taken part in the Paris revolution were admitted.*

for going to sleep and waking up. He often stays up all night and then lies down fully clothed on the sofa at midday and sleeps until evening...'

Having renounced his Prussian citizenship in 1845, Marx could afford to be indifferent to Prussian opinions. But he remained stateless for the rest of his life, being refused British citizenship in 1874.

Marx's only regular source of cash while living in Soho was the payment he received for writing a column on European events for the *New York Daily Tribune*, which he found a bore and a chore – 'newspaper muck'. Engels, who had lodged a few hundred yards away at 6 Macclesfield Street in 1849-50 before moving to Manchester to work in his father's factory, supplemented Marx's income out of his own salary. Marx certainly needed the money. Twice in 1853 he had to pawn his overcoat and three of his five children died while the family was living in Dean Street – he had to borrow the money to pay for a coffin for one of them. To escape creditors he would hide out for weeks with friends in Camberwell or even with Engels in Manchester. Yet he still continued to lend money to others whenever he had any.

Marx's main literary effort while living in Dean Street was focused on the *Eighteenth Brumaire of Louis Napoleon*, a study of French politics which sought to explain the collapse of the Second Republic and its replacement by an authoritarian regime.

In 1856 Jenny Marx inherited two modest legacies which enabled the family to quit what she called their 'evil, frightful rooms' and migrate to Kentish Town and 'a small house at the foot of romantic Hampstead Heath.' They were never to be prosperous but neither were they to endure such wretchedness as they had known in their Soho days.

THE POOR MAN'S GUARDIAN.

BLESSED IS HE THAT CONSIDERETH THE POOR Ps.XLI

No. 6.   SATURDAY, DECEMBER 11, 1847.   PRICE ONE PENNY.

SOUP KITCHEN IN LEICESTER SQUARE.

63. *A soup kitchen in Leicester Square held under the auspices of the Poor Man's Guardian Society and the National Philanthropic Association, in 1847.*

Churches and Chapels

64. St Anne's, Soho, engraving for Chamberlain's History of London, *1770.*

THE PARISH CHURCH

St Anne's was designed either by Sir Christopher Wren or by William Talman – or possibly both, in succession or co-operation. Owing to fund-raising difficulties construction took nearly a decade and the church was not finally consecrated by Henry Compton, the Bishop of London, until 1686. As the Catholic James II had just ascended the throne its dedication was probably a veiled compliment to his staunchly Protestant daughter, the future Queen Anne, who had been Compton's pupil and had recently been betrothed to George, Prince of Denmark. The church organ was acquired as a gift from the Queen's Chapel at St James's Palace, a donation which auspiciously inaugurated a fine musical tradition. The first organist, Dr Croft, was the composer of a well-known hymn tune which he appropriately called *St Anne's*. The spire, by local carpenter John Meard, was not completed until 1718. In the course of the century much was expended on maintenance and decoration, including the acquisition of paintings of Aaron and Moses by Benjamin West.

Nevertheless a major reconstruction was considered essential in 1802 and it was in the course of this work that Meard's steeple was replaced by the distinctive tower designed by Samuel Pepys Cockerell. Its peculiar clock-mounting has been likened to both a Russian 'onion dome' and, less flatteringly, a beer barrel, but Professor Pevsner praises it as 'so remarkable a piece of intransigent early nineteenth century architecture that it must not be allowed to disappear.' In addition to the new tower the church also acquired a new watch-house (from which a guard could view the churchyard to deter grave-robbers), a room for the vestry to meet in and another in which to store the parish fire-engine.

Another major reconstruction was undertaken in 1830-31 and further extensive alterations made in 1866, followed by renovations for Queen Victoria's Golden Jubilee in 1887 and yet more restoration work in 1895-97. The bombing of 1940 destroyed the body of the church, but not the steeple. The site was deconsecrated in 1953 and a major reconstruction as a community centre completed in 1993.

St Anne's musical fame reached its apogee in the last quarter of the nineteenth century, thanks largely to the efforts of Joseph Barnby (1838-96), who inaugurated a series of elaborate musical services and annual performances of Bach's Passion Music in 1871. Despite becoming Director of Music at Eton in 1875 Barnby retained his connection with St Anne's and continued to guide its musical fortunes. In 1886 the choir won the signal acclaim of a summons to Windsor to sing for the Queen. Barnby went on to establish a significant reputation as a composer of sacred music, was knighted and became the second principal of the Guildhall School of Music. His successor as principal, W.H. Cummings, had also served as choirmaster at St Anne's.

65. St Anne's parochial schools in c1879.

66. *The west front of St Anne's, Soho, in 1828.*

67. *Meard Street, watercolour by Stapleton. Named after John Meard, one of the developers of this gem of a street; Meard also designed the spire of St Anne's church.*

68. *St Peter's, Great Windmill Street. From the* Illustrated London News, *20 July 1861.*

OTHER ANGLICAN CHURCHES

St Luke's, Berwick Street originally served as a Huguenot church from 1689 to 1707. Although substantially refurbished at least five times, it was replaced in 1838-9 by a new Decorated Gothic building designed by Edward Blore. It was demolished in 1936.

St Thomas's in Kingly Street was erected in 1702 by Archbishop Tenison as a chapel to serve the needs of the less fashionable part of the parish of St James's, Piccadilly. A small charity school for thirty-six scholars was attached to it. The chapel became a church dedicated to St Thomas in 1869 and in 1871 the school was amalgamated with another of Archbishop Tenison's schools.

St Peter's church in Great Windmill Street was built in 1860-61. Queen Victoria and the Bishop of London were among the subscribers and the foundation stone

was laid by the Earl of Derby, who had subscribed more than a third of the total costs. Lord Salisbury and Gladstone worshipped regularly there. It became an important centre for the reclamation of prostitutes, a cause in which Gladstone was keenly interested. The church was demolished in 1954 but the associated primary school survives.

In 1869 two eighteenth-century houses at 49 and 50 Great Marlborough Street were bought up and a temporary iron church opened behind them. Both it and the houses were demolished in 1884 to make way for a new church in the Perpendicular Gothic style, designed by (Sir) Arthur Blomfield. It was demolished in 1937.

ROMAN CATHOLICS IN SOHO

The Church of Our Lady of the Assumption and St Gregory is London's last surviving example of an eighteenth-century Roman Catholic chapel. Established around 1724 as a private place of worship for the Portuguese Ambassador, it was probably converted from existing outbuildings and stables behind 23-24 Golden Square. Although the priests serving the chapel were technically chaplains to the ambassador and his staff, who enjoyed diplomatic immunity from the penal laws which restricted Catholic worship, in practice their main function was to serve the local English Catholic community. Of forty-four priests who are known to have served there between 1747 and 1783 only three had foreign names.

During the anti-Catholic Gordon riots of 1780 the chapel became a prime target for mob violence. The Bavarian ambassador, by then occupier of the building, managed to save the altar plate and ornaments but most of the rest of the furnishings were dragged into the street and burned before soldiers arrived and the rioters dispersed. The British government paid compensation. The Bavarians left Golden Square and London Catholics built a new church on the site in 1789-90 but it continued to receive Bavarian subventions until that kingdom was absorbed into the German empire in 1871.

ST PATRICK'S

In 1791 Parliament modified long-standing legislative restrictions on Catholic worship and as a result 'a very numerous and respectable body of Catholics conceived the wise and charitable project of establishing a Catholic chapel' near the St Giles's district, which was 'inhabited principally by the poorest and least informed of the Irish who resort to this Country.' To this end they purchased the plain but commodious extension which Mrs Cornelys had erected at the back of Carlisle House as a ballroom and banqueting-house. The leading figure in the enterprise was a witty and learned Irish Franciscan, Father Arthur O'Leary, who preached the first sermon once

69. St Patrick's, Soho Square.

SALEM CHAPEL

This chapel was built behind 8-10 Meard Street in 1824 to accommodate a congregation of Strict Baptists. Its first pastor, John Stevens, was a prolific author of religious books and writer of hymns. In 1878 the congregation moved to a fine new building in Shaftesbury Avenue and for eight years the old premises were used as a warehouse before being taken over by a Baptist missionary organisation and renamed Bloomsbury Hall. In 1907 the building was replaced by a garage.

THE FRENCH PROTESTANT CHURCH

The year 1893 also witnessed the completion of St Patrick's neighbour, the French Protestant Church, built to rehouse the congregation displaced by the demolition of their church in St Martin's le Grand. The new church was designed by (Sir) Aston Webb, who was also responsible for the facade of the Victoria and Albert Museum and that of the Buckingham Palace we know today. Although the new church was intended for French Protestants throughout the London area there were still at that time enough French-

70. Order of Service for the dedication of the new French Protestant Church in Soho Square in 1893.

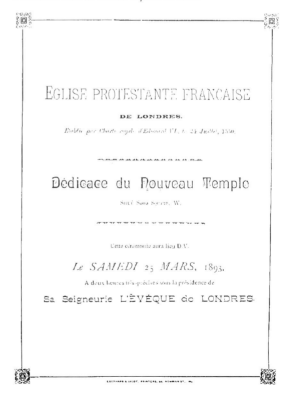

conversion work had been completed in 1792. This outstanding personality was mourned by a congregation of almost two thousand when he died a decade later and for many years the church was generally known as 'Father O'Leary's Chapel'. Father Thomas Barge, who took charge of the church in 1860, worked devotedly among the Irish poor of St Giles and Seven Dials, London's worst rookeries, from which his congregation was largely drawn. He instituted both a temperance society and a Penny Savings Bank but did not live to see the reconstruction of his church in 1891-3. The new red brick church was opened, fittingly, on St Patrick's Day 1893. The frieze on the 125 foot campanile bore a quotation attributed to Ireland's patron saint – *Ut Christiani ita et Romani Sitis* ('As you are children of Christ so be you children of Rome.')

CRAVEN CHAPEL

Opened in 1822 on the site of the former Carnaby Market, this Congregational chapel for two thousand was entirely financed by a retired merchant, Thomas Wilson. It included basement school-rooms, which were replaced in 1874 by a separate Gothic lecture-hall and school. No architectural gem, it subsequently became a factory and warehouse.

71. *The French Protestant Church, Soho Square.*

72. *The Presbyterian Chapel, Little Chapel Street, c1822.*

speakers in Soho itself for the minister of the church, Pasteur Degremont, to hold an open-air service in French on Sunday evenings at the corner of Old Compton Street and Moor Street. A French school, also designed by Webb, was opened in Noel Street in 1898 and continued in use until 1939. During the Second World War the church was much used by 'Free French' servicemen. The congregation today, as well as French, includes Swiss, Belgians, French-speaking citizens of former French colonies and Britons and Americans of Huguenot descent.

THE FRENCH CATHOLIC CHURCH

It was the aptly named Cardinal Wiseman who first foresaw the need for a centrally situated church for French Roman Catholics in London and entrusted the Marist Fathers to realise such a project. Funds were raised principally in France and the lease on the site of Burford's 'Panorama' (see p110) and the adjoin-

ing site was acquired in 1865, when a small chapel was immediately opened in the entrance to the Panorama. A school and an orphanage were established in the house the following year, but the orphanage was transferred to Norwood in 1870 and the school went to Lisle Street in 1890.

The conversion of the Panorama building into a church was entrusted to the French architect Louis-Auguste Boileau (1812-96), who made daring use of iron columns, arches and ribs to create a cruciform space within a circular shell. The first mass was celebrated by Archbishop (later Cardinal) Manning in June 1868.

Severely damaged by bombing in 1940, the church was redesigned by Professor H.O. Corfiato. The first stone, brought from Chartres Cathedral, was laid by the distinguished statesman, M. Maurice Schumann, in 1953 and the completed church opened in 1955. Its special features include an Aubusson tapestry, a mosaic by Boris Anrep and wall-paintings by Jean Cocteau.

Designed by J. Rees.

CROWN STREET CHAPEL

73. *A compilation of texts and scenes issued by the Crown Street Chapel; date unknown.*

74. *The interor of Crown Street Chapel (St Mary the Virgin), 1898.*

75. *The proposed new St Mary the Virgin church in Crown Street, which also included a clergy house and schools, designed by R.H. Carpenter.. The nave was never built. St Martin's School of Art, now amalgamated with Central School, occupies 107-9 Charing Cross Road, where the Greek church (see p35) once stood. From 1682 to 1822, the church, also known as Crown Street Chapel, was in Huguenot hands and became part of a complex of almshouses and school buildings. From 1822 to 1849 a congregation of Calvinistic Independents held sway here before the Church of England acquired the property and refurbished it to the designs of Philip Hardwick as St Mary the Virgin. The congregation was described as numerous but poor, which may explain why further ambitious architectural plans remained unrealised. St Mary's was demolished in 1934 to make way for the art school.*

Crafts, Commerce and Cloth

SILVERSMITHS

In the course of the eighteenth century Soho changed from being an up-market residential area to an increasingly industrial one, though the industries concerned were small-scale, high-skill, luxury trades – silverware, tapestries, furniture, sporting guns, clocks and scientific instruments.

Soho's earliest recorded silversmith was Ellis Gamble of 'Cranbourn Alley, Lester Fields' (illustration 77) who entered his mark at Goldsmiths' Hall in 1696 and took on young William Hogarth as his apprentice in 1712. The Goldsmiths' registers for the years 1698-1739 record twenty-eight names for the Soho area; by the end of the century no less than seventy-five silversmithing businesses had been recorded. Pre-eminent among them were the names of Harache, Lamerie and Garrard – Paul de Lamerie is commemorated by a plaque in Gerrard Street, and Garrard's, now the royal jewellers, have their main premises at the junction of Brewer Street and Regent Street. The industry declined after the 1820s in the face of low-cost competition from Birmingham and Sheffield, though there were still eight firms in the business in the 1890s and another three which specialised in electro-plating and gilding.

76. *Lambert's silversmith's at 10-12 Coventry Street, a handsome Georgian shop, demolished with the rest of the north side of Coventry Street after 1914.*

78. The trade card of Thomas Sheraton, then (c.1795) at 106 Wardour Street. Sheraton's designs were the most influential in a period of remarkable cabinet work. His card advertises not his workshop but his teaching of 'Perspective, Architecture and Ornaments'. It goes on to announce that he sells 'all kinds of Drawing Books' and it is for his publication The Cabinet Makers' and Upholsterers' Drawing Book', *originally issued between 1791 and 1794 in four parts.*

77. The trade card of Ellis Gamble, goldsmith, (in both English and French); his business was at the sign of the Golden Angel in Cranbourn Street. The card was designed and engraved by William Hogarth, his employee.

TAPESTRY AND FURNITURE

After the closure of the Mortlake tapestry workshops in 1703 Soho became the main centre for tapestry manufacture in the capital but the industry failed to outlast the century. Leading Soho craftsmen included Joshua Morris, whose designs characteristically included arabesques, scrollwork, vases, exotic birds etc., Paul Saunders, who concentrated on 'Oriental' motifs and William Bradshaw and George Smith Bradshaw. In 1728 Morris was taken to the Court of Common Pleas by Hogarth for failing to pay up for a tapestry design he had commissioned; the artist sued for thirty pounds and won. Saunders apparently called his premises 'The Royal Tapestry Manufactory, Soho Square'. The *Oxford Companion to the Decorative Arts* summarises the achievement of these craftsmen with a note of mild condescension: 'The products of these Soho workshops, while hardly comparable with the best French tapestries of the period, are of good quality and excellent decorative effect.' Examples of Morris's work can be seen at Hagley Park, near Birmingham and of Saunders' and Bradshaw's at Holkham Hall, Norfolk.

Furniture-making became a significant Soho in-

dustry in the nineteenth century. Sheraton had his workshop in Wardour Street in the 1790s, but within a generation Wardour Street had become synonymous with faked antiques. Cribb and Son of Soho Square, by contrast, enjoyed the prestige of royal patronage and maintained a tradition of craftsmanship from their foundation in 1770 well into the machine age a century later. George Smith of 41 Brewer Street likewise claimed royal patronage and in 1826 described himself as 'Upholsterer and Furniture Draughtsman to His Majesty'; he also published *The Cabinet-Maker's and Upholsterer's Guide, Drawing Book and Repository.* Edwards and Roberts, with premises in Wardour Street, Chapel Street, Dean Street and Carlisle Street, ranked as one of the largest dealers in the country and similarly enjoyed royal patronage, as did the Sinclair Galleries, which specialised in *objets d'art* and occupied five floors at 55 Shaftesbury Avenue. W. & J. Wright of Wardour Street specialised in carving and marquetry while W. & C. Nightingale of Dean Street were specialist manufacturers of bedding.

LEATHER WORKING

Leather-working was another major nineteenth century industry. Almgill & Son of Gerrard Street supplied bridles to the Prince of Wales. Horton's of Lisle Street specialised in making the metal parts for horse harnesses, while their next-door neighbour, appropriately named Mr Leatherby, made the saddle which won first prize at the International Exhibition of 1862. Robson's at the other end of Lisle Street were curriers,

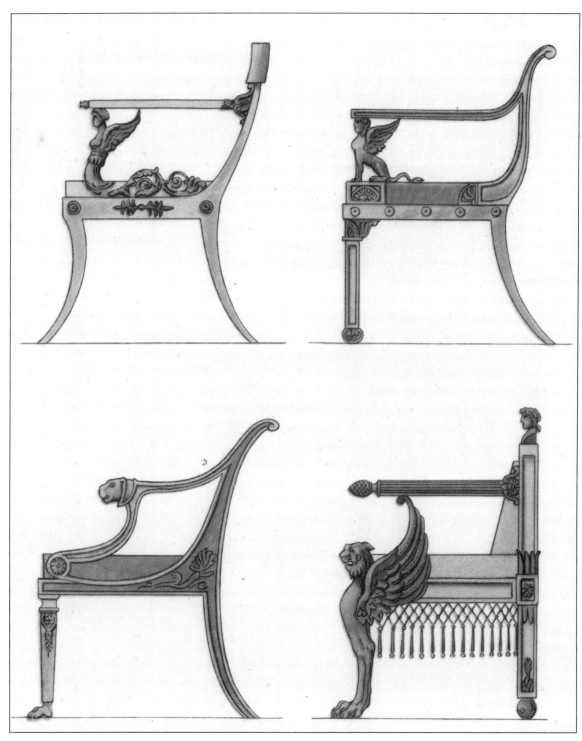

79. *Drawing room chairs, from a coloured engraving in George Smith's* A Collection of Designs for Household Furniture and Interior Decoration, *1808.*

80. Goslett & Co., at 127-131 Charing Cross Road.

who prepared leather for use by other craftsmen. Joseph George of Dean Street specialised in ornamental upholstery and embossed fittings and included Longleat, Knebworth and the Houses of Parliament among his clients. Gamba's the theatrical boot- and shoe-makers, whose clients included Fred Astaire, continued the Dean Street leather-working tradition into the twentieth century.

OTHER SPECIALITIES

A third major employment in the Soho area was the manufacture and sale of glass, represented by Goslett & Co. and Hetley & Co., both of Soho Square, and Ward & Hughes of Frith Street. Hetley & Co. supplied Queen Victoria with glass shades for Windsor Castle and Buckingham Palace, while the business founded by Thomas Ward made windows for

Opening of the Rebuilt Premises
16 Soho Square · London

BILLIARD TABLE BUILDERS
BY
ROYAL APPOINTMENT
ESTD 1845

Messrs. Orme & Sons, Ltd

beg the honour of your inspection of the

British · Field · Sports · Billiard Table

now on View at the above Show-Rooms.

This is the most magnificent Billiard Table
ever built and a perfect object lesson
of British Field Sports.

Addresses
MANCHESTER: BLACKFRIARS ST
GLASGOW: 69 WEST NILE ST
LONDON: 16 SOHO SQUARE
1896

Billiard Tables remodelled & all repairs attended to

81. *A card to mark the opening in 1896 of the rebuilt premises of Orme & Sons, billiard table manufacturers at 16, Soho Square.*

82. *The extensive premises of the tinplate workers, R. and W. Wilson, behind 84-92 Wardour Street.*

Westminster Abbey, the Savoy Chapel, Guildhall and St Anne's, Soho.

In Soho Square, Burroughs & Watts, inventors of the slate-bed billiard table, had premises, with a lesser-known rival, Orme & Sons, in the same square. W.G. Nixey, also of Soho Square, made blacklead and polishes; James Newman of Soho Square, mixed artists' colours, and R. & W. Wilson had a tinplate works which occupied a two acre site between Wardour Street and Dean Street. On the south side of Broadwick Street from 1801 to 1937 stood the Lion Brewery; Trenchard House now occupies its site.

CROSSE AND BLACKWELL

Of the dozens of businesses crammed into Soho a century ago, many boasting royal patronage, one was unrivalled in the eyes of contemporaries:

'Throughout the world Soho Square, though it possesses many other distinctions, is now chiefly known as the place of the principal factories and offices of Messrs. Crosse and Blackwell.' Founded in 1806, this firm of 'Italian Warehousemen' by the end of the century had 2,000 employees, its own wharves at Lambeth and Millwall, a plant in the Caledonian Road producing a million gallons of vinegar a year and at Vauxhall a 'lemon squeezing factory'. The Soho Square premises produced pickles, jam and canned foods. The very model of enlightened capitalists Mr Crosse & Mr Blackwell 'took the lead in discountenancing the dangerous artificial colouring of green fruits and vegetables' provided their workers with a sports ground at Wembley Park and gave generously to local charities. Mr. Blackwell, the Chairman, held practically every parochial office in Soho, became a JP and crowned his career of public service by serving as High Sheriff for Middlesex.

83. The stables of Crosse & Blackwell in Crown Street (today's Charing Cross Road), built in 1876 and designed by R.L. Roumieu. They were demolished when Charing Cross Road was constructed and offices built in their stead. From The Builder, *15 April 1876.*

84.   *Ryders Court off Lisle Street. Crosse & Blackwell commenced business at the small oil and Italian shop at the corner on the right of this sketch by F. Calvert. According to J. Gardner, a noted collector of London material, when he was a boy he daily saw during the season a row of old women sitting in Lisle Street preparing the vegetables or fruit for preserving.*

85. *The offices and works of Crosse & Blackwell in Charing Cross Road in 1904. They were at the corner with Sutton Street, on the site of what became the Astoria Cinema.*

86. A cup and saucer from the service made by Wedgwood for the Empress of Russia, as displayed in Greek Street.

COMMERCE

Given the rival, if routine, retailing attractions of Oxford Street and Regent Street, Soho has often contrived to compete by offering an alternative shopping attraction, something exclusive, or at least off-beat. Three businesses merit special mention.

Josiah Wedgwood maintained his London showrooms at 12 Greek Street from 1774 until 1797. It was the largest house in the street and that shrewd businessman opened it with a flourish, displaying, in five

rooms on two floors, the immense 'Frog' dinner service he had just made to order for Catherine the Great of Russia. It consisted of 952 pieces adorned with 1,244 views. Wedgwood assured his partner that the display would 'bring an immence number of People of Fashion into our Rooms'. It did. Visitors included Queen Charlotte, Prince Ernest of Mecklenburg and the King and Queen of Sweden. Hundreds whose country seats were represented on the service trekked up from the shires to see them. Another royal visit to Greek Street followed in 1779.

Wedgwood knew the sort of area where the fashionable would not feel out of place. So did ex-government contractor John Trotter who, in 1816, opened the Soho Bazaar at 4,5 & 6 Soho Square, to promote 'female and domestic industry' by providing home-workers with an outlet for their products where they could hire under-cover stalls by the day. The goods sold were, indeed, largely the sort of thing women could produce at home–lace, jewellry, gloves, millinery and potted plants. The premises were heated and had their own kitchen and even a dressing-room. The business carried on until 1889.

Liberty's 'Olde World' face in Great Marlborough Street is in distinct contrast to its Regent Street classical frontage and drove the architectural critic, Professor Pevsner to a frenzy of denunciation:

87. Trotter's Bazaar at Nos 4-6 Soho Square in 1819.

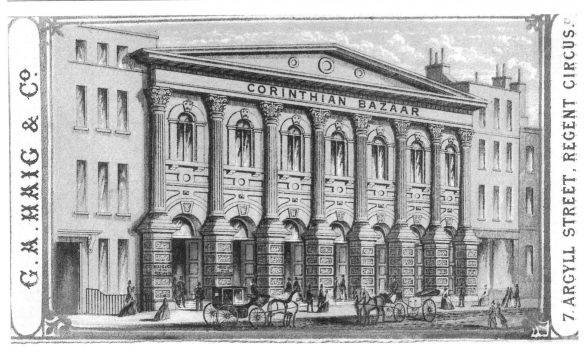

88. *Haig's rival Corinthian bazaar in Argyll Street, c1860-70.*

89. *Liberty's rebuilt premises in Great Marlborough Street; sketch by Hanslip Fletcher.*

90.   *The Italian delicatessen of Camisa & Son at 61 Old Compton Street, a reminder not only of Soho's food speciality, but of the Italian community which is settled there.*

'The timbers are the real article; they come from genuine men-of-war; they are not just stuck on. The roofing-tiles are hand-made, the windows leaded. So technically there is nothing wrong – but functionally and intellectually everything. The scale is wrong, the symmetry is wrong, the proximity to a classical facade....is wrong, and the goings-on of a store behind such a facade (and below those twisted Tudor chimneys) are wrongest of all.'

Apart from the foreign provision and kitchen supplies shops which line Old Compton Street, Soho's other off-beat retail attraction is its street-markets. Carnaby Street epitomised the 'Swinging Sixties' but soon got stuck in its own self-created time-warp. As early as 1968 one of its own shopkeepers complained to a *Sunday Times* reporter that it had ceased to be a showcase for trend-setting fashion and had become 'a tourist attraction – nothing more.' The fact that DJ Simon Dee and film star Faye Dunaway came in November of that year to switch on the Christmas lights rather seemed to confirm this verdict.

Berwick Street market, however, is still definitely a real market – for Londoners. A market that has disappeared, at least in its old form, is Newport Market. Newport Place now centres on a hybrid pagoda-cum-bandstand, but for two centuries it was the site of a market of mixed fortunes. Newport House, built c.1627, once stood here, its gardens stretching over a patch of land with the unappetising name of Scaven-

92. A street seller at Berwick Market.

91. Carnaby Street.

93. *Little Newport Street, at the corner with Lisle Street. Watercolour by J.P. Emslie, 1884.*

ger's Close. The most distinguished inhabitant of this mansion was Mountjoy Blount, Earl of Newport (as in Isle of Wight) who ineptly attempted to align himself with both parties in the Civil War and consequently ended up by being imprisoned, more than once, by both sides. During one of his periods of incarceration the house was occupied by his friend the Earl of Manchester, after he had been sacked as a Parliamentary General. After Blount's death in 1666 the property became the subject of protracted legal dispute until 1682, when it was bought by Nicholas Barbon for £9,500. Characteristically, Barbon used this as security for loans of £30,000, and, having hastily demolished Newport House, let the ground on builders' leases (which brought him another £1,000 a year) and recycled the remains of the mansion to erect a Market House, the profits of which he auctioned off to the Curzons of Kedleston.

Instituted in 1686, Newport Market was held on Tuesdays, Thursdays and Saturdays. Defoe described it in 1725 as one of the chief meat markets of the capital. Rooms above the Market House were occupied by congregations of Huguenots (who referred to it as the *Eglise de la Boucherie*) and then Baptists and, from 1726 to 1729, also provided accommodation for the eccentric 'Orator Henley', whose academy claimed to teach just about anything to just about anyone. The streets leading into the market area were predominantly occupied by goldsmiths, jewellers and clockmakers. Of the surviving buildngs only the upper storeys of 21-24a Newport Court are more or less recognisable in their original state. Although the Market House was rebuilt in the 1830s the area soon became one of the capital's most notorious slums. A well-meaning, high-minded committee, whose members included Gladstone himself, established a 'Newport Market Refuge' to provide 'nightly shelter and sustenance to the really destitute and houseless' and also ran an 'industrial school' for lads who would otherwise be starving, and thieving, on the streets. An attempt to recapitalise and revive the market in 1872 came to nothing. A decade later the area accounted for two-thirds of the arrests in the entire parish of St Anne's and a police report to the Home Secretary declared that 'it would be an act of true philanthropy to break up this reeking home of filthy vice... and remove this festering sore from the centre of London life.' The construction of Charing Cross Road and Shaftesbury Avenue had just that effect.

94. *A shop in Brewer Street; date unknown.*

HAIR CUT & CURLED,
OR WASHED WITH THE PERUVIAN BALM,
LIKEWISE EVERY CONVENIENCE FOR GENTLEMEN TO WASH,

CHARGE **6**D. ONLY

AT

STACEY & Co.'s,
45, *Cranbourn Street, Leicester Square.*

S. & Co. have a large Assortment of

FALSE HAIR,
MADE IN ALL DEVICES,

LADIES' WIGS, from £1 5s. | GENTLEMEN'S WIGS, from £1 1s.

HERBACEOUS BALM
FOR PROMOTING THE GROWTH OF HAIR, 1s. PER BOTTLE.

STRICT ATTENTION TO CLEAN BRUSHES.

95. *The opulence of a hairdressing establishment in the 19th century, and the services provided, displayed in this advertisement for Stacey's at 45 Cranbourn Street.*

96. *Berwick Street Market in the 1920s.*

97. *The market in Rupert Street; painting by E.B. Musman.*

98. Shop in Macclesfield Street, c1900.

CLOTH

Golden Square, which began as an exclusive residential area had by the mid-nineteenth century become dominated by doctors (nine in 1840), hotels and boarding-houses (eight by the 1860s) and solicitors (sixteen in 1870). There were no private residences left, although many of the original buildings still remained largely unaltered – 'residential in aspect if not in occupation', as the *Survey of London* neatly puts it. Over the next forty years, however, Golden Square, so conveniently near to Savile Row, was transformed to become the centre of the woollen and worsted trade in London. There had been a tailor in one or other of the houses in the square since 1777 and Gagniere's, a French house dealing in silk and wool, opened its London office at No. 21 in 1844. In 1868 Messrs Farr and Jones took over No. 12. By 1880 there were ten woollen and worsted merchants in the square, by 1890 forty and by 1900 seventy. In 1914 only four buildings had no connection with the trade and of these one was a glass warehouse, another a piano warehouse and another an hotel. Nineteen of the original thirty-nine domestic dwellings in the square had by then been demolished to make way for office and warehouse buildings. As the *Survey* grievingly notes, 'With a few notable exceptions, they jostle and vie with each other, and the south end, in particular, presents a jagged skyline of ill-assorted gables, a nightmare *Grande Place* effect.'

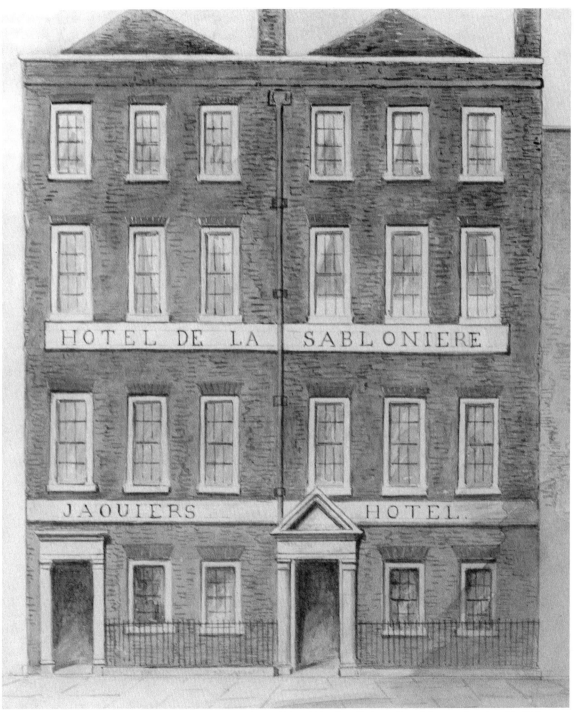

99. *The Sablonière Hotel at Nos. 29-31 Leicester Square from 1788 to 1867, described as a French house where 'a table d'hôte affords the lovers of French cookery and French conversation, an opportunity for gratification at a comparatively moderate charge'. Tourists were to be an important factor in Soho's economy, but the hotels were on the fringe of the area.*

Healers and Hospitals

DOCTORS

Soho has long provided a wide range of therapies – including those prescribed by orthodox medicine – for those troubled in body or mind. Indeed, the area's connection with the medical profession can be said to go back to its very beginnings. One of the earliest residents – of Frith Street and Old Compton Street - was Sir William Waldegrave, personal physician to Mary of Modena, Catholic second wife and Queen to James II.

The distinguished anatomist John Hunter (1728-93) lived at 31 Golden Square from 1763 to 1770 and at 28 Leicester Square from 1783 until his death. Hunter never attempted to qualify as a doctor but learned his trade by preparing dissections for a course in anatomy taught by his elder brother William (1718-83), a celebrated obstetrician. John was subsequently elected surgeon at St George's Hospital, broadened his experience by serving in the army and in 1776 was named Physician Extraordinary to George III. Acknowledged as the founder of pathological anatomy, Hunter was also an indefatigable and fearless experi-

menter. One of his trials involved injecting himself with syphilis to prove that it was a variant form of gonorrhoea. As a result he contracted syphilis, which may explain the maladies and eccentricity of his later years, when he was renowned for both his apoplectic temper and his overweening vanity. (He once told Lord Holland that if he had ever wanted to look at a great man his wish had been granted, for he considered himself a far greater man than Newton.) Despite this, Hunter, more than any other practitioner of his times, helped to raise surgery to the dignity of a profession.

His brother, William Hunter, pioneered the practice of dissection as an essential part of medical training and was appointed Physician Extraordinary to Queen Charlotte in 1762 and first Professor of Anatomy at the Royal Academy in 1768. William lived at 16 Great Windmill Street in a large house which his fellow Scot, Robert Malone, adapted to provide him with not only a residence but also a library, lecture theatre, dissecting rooms and museum for his 10,000 anatomical specimens. The specimens were removed to Glasgow University in 1807 but medical lectures continued there until 1831, after which the building became a printing works, then the Hotel de L'Etoile and, after 1887, part of the Lyric Theatre.

John Hunter is commemorated by a portrait bust in Leicester Square, Dr John Snow, the first royal anaesthetist, by the more substantial memorial of a public

100. John Hunter; oil painting by J. Jackson

101. William Hunter.

house – a singularly inappropriate accolade for a vegetarian teetotaller. Snow's claim on posterity is the result of a brilliantly original work of medical detection.

When London was visited by cholera in 1854 it claimed ten thousand victims, including more than 120 in Broad (now Broadwick) Street alone. In a pioneering contribution to epidemiology, Snow mapped the distribution of fatalities in Soho and, by doing so, traced the source of infection to a pump in Broad Street. He had the handle removed. When news was brought of the subsequent death of a victim in Hampstead, miles away, Snow's hypothesis seemed challenged - until it was revealed that the victim, a former Sohoite, had drunk water fetched specially from that very same pump. The public house named in Snow's honour now occupies its site.

INSTITUTIONS

After the death of Alderman Beckford his house at 22 Soho Square was taken by Dr George Armstrong as premises for his Dispensary for Sick Children. This pioneer paediatrician strongly opposed parting sick

102. The public house in BroadwickStreet named after Dr John Snow.

children from their parents, believing it far better to prescribe for them from a dispensary than put them in hospitals, where the risk of secondary infections was far greater than at home. Supported by charitable subscribers, Armstrong gave both treatment and medicines free, three times a week. By the time financial difficulties had forced him to relinquish Soho Square he had treated over thirty thousand patients. The dispensary moved to Seven Dials but closed in 1781 after Armstrong was felled by a stroke.

From 1774 onwards the medical needs of Soho's local population were dealt with by the Westminster General Dispensary, housed until 1825 at 33 Gerrard Street and then at 9 Gerrard Street, in the building

103. The Westminster General Dispensary at 9 Gerrard Street.

104. The Heart and Paralysis Hospital at 32 Soho Square.

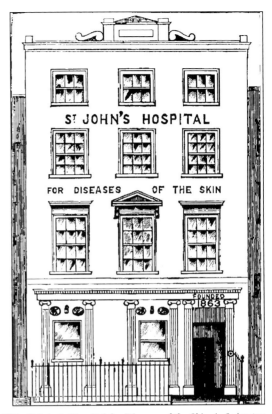

105. St John's Hospital for Diseases of the Skin, in Leicester Square.

formerly occupied by the Turk's Head, the original meeting-place of Johnson's 'Club'. The Dispensary, supported by charitable subscriptions, was intended to provide 'Advice and Medicines to such useful Persons as support themselves by their Industry when in Health, but are utterly unable to struggle with the Expenses of Sickness; and cannot, without injury to their private Affairs, leave their Habitations to receive the Benefit of other Institutions.' This innovation must have been a welcome one as Soho cannot claim to have been a particularly salubrious district. The St Anne's Burial Register for the years around 1800 reveals high rates of infant mortality and small-pox fatalities, as well as individual deaths attributed to 'St Anthony's Fire', 'Yellow Gaunders', 'Watery Gripes' and 'Gin Fever'.

Soho has, perhaps surprisingly in the light of the above, nevertheless been home to one of the highest concentrations of specialised medical institutions in the capital.

The Royal Ear Hospital, first established at 10 Dean Street in 1816 as the Royal Dispensary for Diseases of the Ear, was relocated in Frith Street in 1876, returned to 42/3 Dean Street in 1904 and then removed to Huntley Street in 1927. It claimed to be 'the oldest

Institution for the special treatment of Aural and allied Diseases, not only in this country, but in Europe.'

The foundation of the Royal Dental Hospital dates from 1858 and from 1860 to 1873 was housed at 32 Soho Square in the former home of Sir Joseph Banks. It was then occupied from 1874 to 1913 by the National Hospital for Diseases of the Heart and Paralysis. The Dental Hospital, meanwhile, moved to 40/1 Leicester Square, although its buildings, now the Hampshire Hotel on Leicester Square, date from 1901. Kent's *Encyclopaedia of London* records that in 1935 37,348 teeth were extracted there.

The London Lock Hospital was founded in 1746 but did not establish itself in Soho until 1862. It specialised in the treatment of venereal diseases, treating over 22,000 out-patients a year by the 1890s, 90% of them male. A contemporary summary of its work noted that 'The Hospital receives patients from all parts of the kingdom. Every precaution is taken to prevent the charity becoming an encouragement to vice.' A Chaplain, assisted by a male and a female 'missionary', gave spiritual reinforcement to the healing process.

106. *St John's Hospital for Diseases of the Skin in Lisle Street. This striking building stands on the site of the home of General Oglethorpe, founder of Georgia. In its present form the building dates from 1897.*

107. The Hospital for Women in Soho Square.

Another specialist institution was St John's Hospital for Diseases of the Skin, founded in 1863. From 1865 to 1887 it was housed at 45 Leicester Square and from 1887 to 1935 at 49 Leicester Square; it offered a confidential evening service for the 'artisan classes' who might have jeopardised their employment had the nature of their affliction become known to their employers. The distinctive building which it occupied from 1936 onwards dates from 1897. Built on the site of the former home of General Oglethorpe, founder of Georgia, it originally housed the French Club and subsequently the film-makers Pathé of France and Pathescope Limited. An allied institution was the West London Dispensary for Diseases of the Skin, which was at 60 Poland Street from 1867 to 1883 and at 61 from 1884 until 1896.

Another specialist centre was the Free Dispensary for Throat Diseases which took over 32 Golden Square in 1865 and replaced it with a purpose-built building in 1882. It later became the Royal National Ear, Nose and Throat Hospital.

Specialist treatment for women was prefigured by the establishment in Dean Street of Queen Adelaide's Lying-In Hospital but this was only one of a number of similar institutions devoted to childbirth. In 1843 The Hospital for Diseases of Women was founded in Red Lion Square by Dr Protheroe Smith, then Assistant Lecturer on Midwifery and Diseases of Women at St Bartholomew's Hospital. It changed its name in 1845 to The Hospital for Women as the original name discouraged potential subscribers who thought it only treated venereal diseases. It moved to larger premises in Soho Square in 1851 as 'the first institution established in this or any other country exclusively for the treatment of those maladies which neither rank, wealth nor character avert from the female sex.' It became a pioneering centre for teaching and research, as well as treating over 170,000 patients in the first half century of its existence. Despite its amalgamation with the Middlesex Hospital when the National Health Service was established the inscription above its building still proclaims its unambiguous claim to be 'THE Hospital for Women'.

Bourgeois Bohemians

In *Vanity Fair* Thackeray locates the home of Becky Sharp and her wastrel father in Greek Street, less than a mile – and a thousand miles – from the elegance of Russell Square. Sir Thomas Lawrence (1769-1830) made that actual transition.

If Soho has had more than its share of Bohemian artists it has also been home to a number of bourgeois ones.

William Hogarth (1697-1764) lived at 30 Leicester Square from 1733 until his death. Poverty had obliged him initially to train as an engraver and set up as a producer of bill-heads, trade-cards and book-illustrations, studying painting in his spare time, first at the St Martin's Lane Academy and subsequently under his future father-in-law, Sir James Thornhill. Hogarth's own master, Ellis Gamble, and the silversmith Paul de Lamerie were among his early clients. By using the skills he had acquired as a youthful engraver Hogarth was later able to see reproductions of his paintings to a mass-market, thus freeing himself from depend-

109. *William Hogarth's trade card, designed and engraved by himself, at the Golden Ball, on the corner of 'Cranborne Alley [and] Little Newport Street', 1720.*

ence on dealers and their dilettante clientele.

Hogarth first won popular acclaim with scenes from John Gay's hugely successful *Beggar's Opera* (1728) and went on to build much of his career around similar portrayals of London life from a satirical and moralistic point of view: 'I have endeavoured to treat my subjects as a dramatic writer; my picture is my stage, and men and women my players.' As the essayist Charles Lamb asserted almost a century later 'other pictures we look at – his prints we read.'

Hogarth spotted what later generations were to call 'a gap in the market' – 'modern moral subjects, a field not broken up in any country and any age. The reasons which induced me to adopt this mode of designing were, that I thought both writers and painters had, in the historical style, totally overlooked that intermediate species of subject which may be placed between the sublime and the grotesque.'

Widespread pirating of Hogarth's work prompted the artist to secure the passage in 1735 of 'Hogarth's Act', by which Parliament gave statutory protection to an artist's copyright in his work. Hogarth held back publication of the eight-part print cycle depicting *The Rake's Progress* until the day this legislation came into force.

A more than competent portraitist, Hogarth lacked the willingness to flatter which might have brought him greater eminence and fortune. One of his finest portraits (illustration 111) depicts Thomas Coram, founder of the Foundling Hospital, of which Hogarth was an enthusiastic and generous patron. Coram was a near neighbour of Hogarth's, living in Panton Street (then known as Spur Street).

Thackeray summarised Hogarth as 'a jovial, honest London citizen, stout and sturdy; a hearty, plain-spoken man, loving his laugh, his friends, his roast beef of old England, and having a proper bourgeois

108. *William Hogarth, by G.M. Brighty. Published 1817 by C.G. Dyer of 'Compton Street, Soho'.*

110. *'The Rake's Progress', Plate VI, by Hogarth.*

scorn for French frogs, for mounseers ...foreign fiddlers, foreign singers and, above all, for foreign painters, whom he held in the most amusing contempt.' Hogarth's sole foray into France confirmed all his prejudices, not least when his casual sketching got him arrested as a spy. His revenge was *Calais Gate, or The Roast Beef of Old England*, which portrays the French as priest-ridden wretches. Hogarth's Francophobia has been much remarked on by his biographers; less often do they remember that if ever he wanted to hone his dislike of the French all he had to do was to stroll round the corner from his house.

Hogarth must have been aware of the nearby presence of that most successful of foreign interlopers, his exact contemporary Antonio Canal (1697-1768), better known to posterity as Canaletto, who lodged with Richard Wiggan, cabinet-maker, at 41 Beak Street (then 16 Silver Street) in 1749-51. The prolific Venetian

had prospered by selling picturesque views of his native city to English milords passing through on their 'Grand Tour'. The war of the Austrian succession severely dented his trade and its cessation in 1748 prompted him to hasten to London to repair his fortunes. While in Beak Street he placed a newspaper advertisement inviting 'any Gentleman that will be pleased to come to his House, to see a Picture done by him, being *A View of St James's Park* – which now hangs in the Tate Gallery, courtesy of Sir Andrew Lloyd Webber, who bought it at auction for £10,000,000.

If Hogarth aimed to affirm the independence of the artist as craftsman, Sir Joshua Reynolds (1723-92) sought to raise him to the level of a gentleman. He certainly succeeded in his own case, becoming *Sir Joshua* and first President of the newly-established Royal Academy. Devonian by birth, Reynolds was

111. Captain Thoms Coram, portrait by William Hogarth. Coram, founder of the Foundling Hospital, was a friend and neighbour of Hogarth.

Birkbeck, Burdett, Place, Campbell and other radicals for 'the Diffusion of Useful Knowledge among Persons engaged in Commercial and Professional Pursuits.' Charles Goodyear, inventor of vulcanized rubber, occupied the premises from 1856 to 1859 and they then passed to auctioneers Puttick and Simpson until 1937, when they were demolished to allow for the extension of the AA's headquarters, Fanum House.

Reynolds' protégé, the Swiss Angelica Kauffmann (1740-1807), lived at 16 Golden Square from 1767 until 1781, when she married her second husband, the painter Antonio Zucchi. A founder member of the Royal Academy, even though it was established only two years after her arrival in London, she was frequently employed to decorate interiors, and especially ceilings, in houses being built within a few hundred yards of her home, at Portman Square, Bedford Square and Berkeley Square.

One could scarcely imagine a greater contrast of personalities than between the genteel Angelica and the vulgar, eccentric but highly talented sculptor Joseph Nollekens (1737-1823) who was born at 29 Dean Street, the son of a painter. He could turn his hand from erotica to portrait busts to funerary monuments and was equally adept at copying and repairing the work of others. A notorious skinflint, he left a fortune of £200,000. Nollekens' only serious rival, John Flaxman (1755-1826) lived in Poland Street and

112. Angelica Kauffmann.

initially apprenticed to a friend of Hogarth's, the facile but commercially successful portraitist, Thomas Hudson. After studying in Italy, Reynolds settled initially in lodgings in St Martin's Lane but was soon able to take a large house in Great Newport Street (1754-60), before moving to 47 Leicester Square, where he lived until his death. He found the house 'though large and respectable, still insufficient for his professional purposes' and spent almost as much as he had paid for it on an extension which provided him with a twenty-foot octagonal painting-room and a detached gallery in which to exhibit his works.

Numbering Dr Johnson and David Garrick among his friends, Reynolds became not only the foremost painter of his day but also a figure of consequence in society, until failing eyesight and hearing clouded his final years. Reynolds' *Discourses* became a classic statement of the classical notion of good taste, epitomised in the notion that 'the whole beauty and grandeur of art consists in being able to get above all singular forms, local customs, particularities and details of every kind.'

After Reynolds' death his house passed to his niece and house-keeper, who married a sixty-six-year-old Earl, 'a six-bottle man'. It later served as a tailor's and draper's and then (1828-52) as home to the Western Literary and Scientific Institution, founded by

113. *A lecture at the Western Literary and Scientific Institution in Sir Joshua Reynold's old house at 47 Leicester Square.*

Wardour Street as a young man. Throughout his Soho sojourn he was much employed in making designs for Wedgwood, whose London showroom was in nearby Greek Street.

Reynolds' successor as President of the Royal Academy was the American, Benjamin West (1738-1820), who lived in Panton Square from 1768 to 1775 before moving to a large house and studio in Newman Street, just north of Soho. His protégé and fellow-countryman, John Singleton Copley (1738-1815), lived at 28 Leicester Square from 1774 until 1783, during which period he was elected to the Royal Academy and painted *The Death of Chatham* (National Portrait Gallery) and *The Death of Major Peirson* (Tate Gallery) a huge, dramatic depiction of the repulse of French troops from Jersey, which won immense acclaim. Copley, despite this success, sadly declined into debt and dementia.

Unlike Hogarth or Reynolds or Copley, who were drawn to Soho, William Blake (1757-1827) was born there at 28 (later 74) Broadwick Street, where he passed most of his childhood. In 1784 he set up at Number 27 (then 72) as a print-seller but removed to 28 Poland Street the following year and stayed there until 1791. He possessed – or was possessed by – a turbulent and individual genius so impatient with the conventional boundaries of knowledge that he is now venerated as a strikingly original talent in both art and literature. Wordsworth thought him mad, but found his madness more interesting than the sanity of Scott or Byron. Of later poets de la Mare, Auden, Housman, Eliot, Yeats and Ginsberg have all written in his praise. His painterly disciples range from Samuel Palmer to Paul Nash.

Entering the Royal Academy Schools at twenty-one Blake did not take to the urbane suavity of its presiding spirit as his subsequent 'Annotations to Reynolds' *Discourses* unambiguously convey:

'Having spent the Vigour of my Youth and Genius under the Oppression of Sr Joshua & his Gang of Cunning Hired Knaves Without Employment & as much as could possibly be Without Bread, The Reader must expect to Read in all my Remarks on these Books Nothing but Indignation and Resentment.'

As an artist Blake rated himself below Michelangelo, Raphael and Dürer but above Titian, Rubens and

114. Joseph Nollekens

115. William Blake on Hampsted Heath, by John Linnell.

Rembrandt. His nonconformity in politics, morality and religion undoubtedly cost him material success but won him the devoted friendship of such artists as Flaxman and the Swiss exile Henry Fuseli, who paid him the ambiguous compliment of being 'damned good to steal from!'.

Believing that 'if the doors of perception were cleansed everything would appear as it is, infinite.' Blake was driven by the desire to translate his mystical visions into precise visual form and so experimented ceaselessly with novel techniques of printing and painting, using line with great precision but using colour non-naturalistically. Hazlitt opined that 'he is ruined by vain struggles to get rid of what presses on his brain – he attempts impossibles.' Blake's self-imposed quest was summarised in one of his own couplets:

'To see a World in a Grain of Sand,
And Heaven in a Wild Flower.'

Blake's advertisement for an exhibition of his own works (in Carnaby Street) was truculent in its defiance:

'The ignorant insults of individuals will not hinder me from doing my duty to my Art ...and those who have been told that my works are but an unscientific and irregular eccentricity, a madman's scrawls, I

demand of them to do me the justice to examine before they decide.'

Posterity's judgment has assigned a substantial selection of Blake's work to a place of honour in the Tate Gallery – in a separate room from the works of Sir Joshua.

Dissent was the hallmark of Blake's notoriety, dissolution of George Morland's (1763-1804). An archetypal drunk, this offspring of painter Henry Robert Morland (1719-97), was exhibiting at the Royal Academy while still a teenager. He progressed to forging Dutch landscapes and squandered his undoubted talent by churning out rustic scenes and coastal landscapes which found a ready market and therefore kept him in drink. He lived intermittently with John Harris, publisher of his sketch-books, at 29 Gerrard Street, and with his brother Henry, proprietor of Morland's Hotel in Dean Street, who probably endured him less from fraternal duty than for the opportunity to deal in his works. Despite his abject failure Morland received the sincere testimony of his artistic contemporaries in being consistently copied and faked.

While Blake and Morland were, in their different ways, defying convention and paying the price, the future Sir Thomas Lawrence (1769-1830) was embel-

116. *George Morland.*

117. *Benjamin Haydon; pencil and chalk drawing by G.H. Harlow, 1816.*

lishing it and reaping the reward. A self-taught child prodigy, Lawrence was nevertheless a devoted disciple of Reynolds in his attitudes both to painting and patrons. Graduating from fashionable Bath to London, he settled at 60 Greek Street while still only 21 and was elected to the Royal Academy at 25. He succeeded Reynolds as the leading society portraitist of the day and moved on to newly-built, ultra-smart Russell Square in 1814. On the death of Benjamin West in 1820 he succeeded him as President of the Royal Academy. Both talent and personality suited him to serve as figurehead of his profession, as a contemporary recorded:

'His manner was elegant, but not high bred. He had too much that air of always submitting. He had smiled so often and so long, that at last his smile wore the appearance of being set in enamel.'

The writer of those lines was Benjamin Haydon (1786-1846), another devotee of Reynolds and the 'Grand Manner'. The fact that he is chiefly remembered as a diarist is perhaps the most apt comment on his status as an artist. Wordsworth, Lamb and Keats all admired his work but Hazlitt, on being shown Haydon's *Judgment of Solomon*, enquired bitchily 'Why did you paint it so large? A small canvas might have

concealed your faults.' Haydon lived at 46 Great Marlborough Street from 1808 to 1817. The archetype of the frustrated Romantic genius, he ended dismally, committing suicide to escape his debts and abandoning a wife and young family to their fate.

Another artist more remembered for his writing than his painting was James Northcote (1746-1831) who lived at 8 Argyll Place from 1790 to 1831. He wrote biographies of Reynolds and Titian, two series of 'Fables' and memoirs (*Conversations*) which recount his acquaintance with the artists and writers of his day.

Between the time of Hogarth and Haydon Soho was home to literally hundreds of artists, albeit fleetingly for many. Dean Street alone numbered among its residents the painter Beechey, the caricaturist Cruikshank, the sculptor Behnes and the architect Thomas Hardwick, while Frith Street could boast the Royal Drawing Master, J.A. Gresse and for the year 1810-11, Constable himself. Other Soho denizens have included the architects Gibbs, Inwood, Leoni, Chambers and Norman Shaw and the painters Sandby, Cotman, Romney and Zoffany, not to mention legions of obscure water-colourists, engravers, drawing-masters and makers of picture-frames.

Living off Letters

Soho's literary tradition goes back virtually to its beginnings when diarist John Evelyn (1620-1706) took his family to spend the winter in 'the great Square' at Soho. Other short-term literary residents include Shelley, who lodged at 11 Poland Street in 1811 after his expulsion from Oxford, Johnson's biographer Boswell, who lodged at 22 Gerrard Street in 1775 and 1776 and the South African poet Roy Campbell, who lived at 50 Beak Street (1920-2) after getting married at the age of nineteen.

THE SATIRIST AND THE SCEPTIC

John Dryden (1631-1700) lived for the last fourteen years of his life at 44 Gerrard Street, then but newly-built, and died there of gout and gangrene. The plays he wrote in his ground floor room are all but forgotten but his *Song for St Cecilia's Day* (1687) has been much anthologised and his translation of Virgil was hailed as a masterpiece. A brilliant versifier, a discerning critic and a savage satirist, Dryden has been called 'the literary dictator of his age' and was praised by Congreve, Pope and Johnson. The *Cambridge Guide to English Literature* hails him as the first master of 'modern English prose' and 'a professional in the

modern sense of the word'. But, if Dryden won admirers, he also made enemies. In 1679 he was mercilessly beaten up by three thugs in Covent Garden; who paid them and why remains a mystery. Having got away with praising both Cromwell and Charles II, Dryden converted to Catholicism at the height of an outbreak of Protestant bigotry and remained doggedly loyal to James II, though it cost him many posts of profit and honour, including the Laureateship.

Nor could Dryden look for consolation in his domestic life, for his wife accused him of preferring musty old books to her company and vowed to change herself into a library volume to get her due share of attention. The poet revenged himself in her epitaph:

'Here lies my wife : here let her lie!
Now she's at rest, and so am I.'

Dryden himself lies with Chaucer in Westminster Abbey's Poets Corner. In 1863 he became the first person to gain the accolade of a London street wall plaque. Unfortunately the Society of Arts put it on the wrong house – No.43 – now a Chinese supermarket.

Scottish philosopher and historian David Hume (1711-1776) lived at 40 Brewer Street from 1767 to 1769, following in the footsteps of a fellow Scot, novelist Tobias Smollett, who lived in the same street in 1765. Belated fame had come to Hume through his

119. Dryden's house in Gerrard Street.

118. John Dryden

120. David Hume.

121. Thomas De Quincey.

eight volume *History of Great Britain*, which remained a standard work for nearly a century and ran to almost two hundred editions. The writings of the philosopher reveal the mind of an austere sceptic but the portrait of the man, by another Scot, Allan Ramsay, shows a corpulent, genial 'turtle-eating Alderman'. Hume's metropolitan sojourn was a consequence of his appointment as Under Secretary of State but he disliked London and returned with relief to a new house in Edinburgh, consoling himself with the ironic observation that his writings had made him 'no enemies, except indeed, all the Whigs, all the Tories, and all the Christians.

DEATH, DELIVERANCE AND DRAMATICS

No. 6 Frith Street was the last home of the prolific essayist and critic William Hazlitt (1778-1830). Combining extensive knowledge with originality of judgment, he could write as perceptively about the theatre or painting as about poetry or novels; but he was not always the best judge of where to direct his efforts. An unrepentant admirer of the French Revolution, he devoted much of his later years to a massive *Life of Napoleon*, despite the fact that most of his countrymen regarded the would-be master of Europe as a bloodstained tyrant. Divorced in 1822 and arrested for debt in 1823, Hazlitt was abandoned by his second wife in

1827. The inveterate walker became a recluse. The last months of his life are chronicled in an essay aptly entitled 'The Sick Chamber'. His death was variously attributed to excessive tea-drinking and 'a species of cholera', and his last words were 'Well, I've had a happy life.' His burial, at St. Anne's, Soho, was attended by two mourners.

Soho dealt more kindly with Thomas De Quincey (1785-1859), though it might scarcely have seemed so at the time. The clever son of a prosperous merchant, he ran away from Manchester Grammar School, drifted through Wales and finally pitched up in Soho. By his own account he would have starved but for the kindness of Ann, a prostitute scarcely older than himself, whom he met in Soho Square. She disappeared one day into a London crowd and he never saw her again, though she haunted his dreams to the end of his days. Their friendship became the basis of a vivid episode in his autobiographical *Confessions of an Opium Eater* (1822), the book that made his reputation as a writer.

No. 49 Frith Street was, from 1821 to 1829, the home of Mary Russell Mitford (1787-1855) and an uncompromisingly urban setting in which to complete *Our Village: Sketches of Rural Life, Character and Scenery*, which began as a series of contributions to *The Lady's Magazine* in 1819 and subsequently appeared in five volumes. The author's Soho residence makes more sense in the light of her dramatic output. *Julian*, with the great Macready in the title role, was produced successfully at Covent Garden in 1823 and followed by the even more successful *Foscari* in 1826 and *Rienzi* in 1828. A warm, gossipy, life-loving person, she corresponded extensively with Lamb, Ruskin and Elizabeth Barrett Browning.

THE BOOK TRADE

Soho's connections with the book trade probably arose less from the presence of a few eminent writers than from its convenient location between scholarly Bloomsbury on the one hand and the commerce of the West End on the other. Booksellers, printers and publishers have played a continuing role in Soho life for over two centuries. Many concentrated on some specialist aspect of the market. Mitchell & Hughes, established in Wardour Street in 1797, excelled in the printing of pedigrees and family histories and pioneered the publication of the works of the Swedish mystic, Emanuel Swedenborg; Pettit & Cox of Old Compton Street became leading suppliers of business diaries; Howlett & Son of Frith Street specialised in printing in gold - everything from menus and opera programmes to labels for boxes of patent pills; Kimpton's of Wardour Street was, in the mid nineteenth century, one of only three specialist medical booksellers in the whole of London. Bookshops, of course, now line the sides of Charing Cross Road, a thoroughfare renowned for its number of new, secondhand and remainder stores. The road was at one time synonymous with the large shop established by the Foyle brothers, William and Gilbert, who were sufficiently encouraged by the sale of their redundant textbooks to set up a bookselling business that began in Cecil Court between Charing Cross Road and St Martin's Lane, and had grown so large by 1929 when new premises were opened that the Lord Mayor was in attendance. The specialist tradition was continued into the present century by the establishment in 1923 of David Garnett's Nonesuch Press at 30 Gerrard Street. Aiming to produce only books of the highest

122. *William Hazlitt.*

quality in both content and presentation it took twelve years to publish its first one hundred titles.

Soho Square became especially notable for its publishers. Dulau and Company, founded by a Benedictine refugee from the French Revolution, prospered on the sale of textbooks of the French master at Eton and Baedeker's classic tourist guides. Routledge enjoyed such a huge success with Harriet Beecher Stowe's *Uncle Tom's Cabin* that in 1860 they removed to Ludgate Hill. In modern times the Square became the London base of two leading Scottish publishers, Chambers, and A. & C. Black and of the personable Rupert Hart-Davis.

Music and Musicians

THE SOUND OF MUSIC

'Those Ladies and Gentlemen who will honour him with their Company from Twelve to Three in the afternoon, any Day in the Week... may, by taking a Ticket, gratify their Curiosity, and not only hear this young Music Master and his Sister perform in private; but likewise try his surprising Musical Capacity, by giving him any thing to play at Sight, or any Music without Bass, which he will write upon the Spot, without recurring to his Harpsichord. (*The Public Advertiser*, March 1765.)

The young 'Music Master' in question was Wolfgang Amadeus Mozart, then on the final stage of a year-long European tour. Taking lodgings at the home of a stay-maker at 20 Frith Street, the Mozarts gave their public performances in Caldwell's Assembly Rooms

at 21 Dean Street and at the Hickford Rooms at 63-65 Brewer Street, which claimed to be the capital's premier concert venue. During his time in Soho Mozart, then aged nine, composed his first symphony – the 'London'.

Other distinguished musical visitors to Soho have included Haydn, Wagner and Johann Strauss. Haydn took what he thought 'charming and comfortable, but very expensive lodgings' at 18 Great Pulteney Street in 1791-2. Here he wrote six of the 'Salomon' symphonies, occasionally peering out in wonder at fog so thick 'you could spread it on bread'.

Wagner, then an obscure conductor with an appalling employment record, stayed for a week in Old Compton Street in August 1839, recuperating from a horrendous Baltic voyage, the memories of which inspired *The Flying Dutchman*. In vain he attempted to arrange an appointment with Lord Lytton, whose

123. The child prodigy – Wolfgang Amadeus Mozart

124. No 20 Frith Street, where the Mozart family stayed during their visit to London in 1764-5.

125. *Hickford's Rooms at 63-5 Brewer Street, once London's premier music venue.*

novel *Rienzi* he had adapted for the opera. In the same year Johann Strauss made his first triumphant visit to London, putting up in style at the German Hotel in Leicester Place – which, as Manzi's, still provides convenient accommodation for music technicians working in nearby dubbing studios.

Musical entertainment in Soho predates Mozart by at least half a century. In 1710 Z. C. von Uffenbach visited the Turk's Head (then known as the Romer tavern) in Gerrard Street, where 'the host, a Frenchman called Binet, holds a weekly concert'. At 35 Golden Square the occupant from 1710 to 1724, Thomas Robinson, 'established weekly concerts and assemblies in the manner of *conversazione* which were frequented by all such as had any pretensions to politeness and good taste'; their chief, scarcely veiled, object was to show off Robinson's daughter, Anastasia, a celebrated singer. Handel's oratorios were performed 'at the Great House in Thrift [Frith] Street, Soho, (late the Venetian Ambassador's)', where the audience were assured that they would be 'kept in proper Warmth by the Help of a German stove, to prevent them from catching Cold.'

126. *A ticket to 'admit a Lady' to the Philharmonic Society concert at Hickford's Rooms in Brewer Street in the later 18th century.*

127. *The interior of Hickford's Great Room.*

128. *Dr Charles Burney.*

129. *Vincent Novello.*

THE BUSINESS OF MUSIC

In the same year that Wagner and Strauss were staying in Soho Dickens published *Nicholas Nickleby*, whose description of Golden Square confirms it as a quintessentially musical locality:

'Two or three violins and a wind instrument from the Opera band reside within its precincts. Its boarding-houses are musical, and the notes of pianos and harps float in the evening time past the head of the mournful statue, the guardian genius of a little wilderness of shrubs, in the centre of the square. On a summer's night, windows are thrown open and groups of swarthy mustachio'd men are seen by the passer-by lounging at the casements, and smoking fearfully. Sounds of gruff voices practising vocal music invade the evening's silence, and the fumes of choice tobacco scent the air. There, snuff and cigars, and German pipes and flutes and violins, and violincellos, divided the supremacy between them. It is the region of song and smoke. Street bands are on their mettle in Golden Square, and itinerant glee-singers quaver involuntarily, as they raise their voices within its boundaries.'

The music industry was already a century old in Soho by the time that passage was written. Handel's amanuensis, John Christopher Smith, lived at 6 Carlisle Street from 1756 until his death in 1763. His former home now houses the offices of *Private Eye*. Dr Charles Burney (1726-1814), the celebrated musicologist, lived at 50 Poland Street from 1760 until 1770.

The harpsichord maker, Jacob Kirkman, was established at 17 Great Pulteney Street from 1739 to 1750 when he moved to 54 Broadwick Street, where the business continued until 1832. Burckhardt Tschudi and his son-in-law John Broadwood, and then their successors, ran the same business at No. 32 from 1743 until 1904. In the 1790s the Italian composer Domenico Corri and his son-in-law, the Czech J. L. Dussek, ran a combined music-publishing and musical instrument business at 90 Dean Street. The organ builders, Bevington and Sons, began business in Manette Street around 1794. Over the course of the next century they built some 2,000 organs, including those at St Paul's, Covent Garden and St Martin-in-the-Fields. By the mid-eighteenth century at least four violin-makers were active in Soho, which thus became the capital's chief centre for the manufacture and sale of stringed instruments, under the dominant leadership of the Hill, Hart, Lott, Tubbs and Panormo family businesses. As late as the 1890s there were no less than eight Soho firms making or dealing in violins and covering the whole spectrum of the business, from one which imported fine Stradivarius instruments, to another which yearly exported hundreds of 'dilapidated fiddles' to Chicago for refurbishment and an unknown fate on the frontier.

NOVELLO'S

In 1811 Vincent Novello, music professor and organist of the Portuguese Embassy chapel published a *Collection of Sacred Music* at his own expense and in 1813 he became a founder-member of the London Philharmonic Society. In 1829 Novello's son, Alfred, established a modest music-publishing business at 67 Frith Street, beginning with an issue of Purcell's *Sacred Music*. Mendelssohn and Charles Lamb were frequent guests at the family's musical evenings. By 1834 the business had moved to 69 Dean Street; by 1845 there was a branch of Novello's at 24 Poultry in the City and in 1852 another on Broadway in New York. Novello's grew and prospered by using new printing technology to 'Make trivial price of serious things' (a marketing tag filched from Shakespeare) and by encouraging the formation and ambitions of choral societies through a monthly publication, the *Musical Times*. In 1860 Novello first issued *Hymns Ancient and Modern*, a mainstay of Protestant liturgy for a century to come. In the 1890s the company moved its printing and book-binding activities into a purpose-built block, designed by Frank Loughborough Pearson and flanked by Hollen Street and Little Chapel (now Sheraton) Street on the east side of Wardour Street. In 1905-6 the same architect designed a handsome new head office, modelled on the town hall of Bremen, at 152-60 Wardour Street. The main staircase was fittingly adorned with the statue of Handel made in 1738 by Roubiliac for the Vauxhall

130. An interior of the headquarters of the Royal Society of Musicians at 11-13 Lisle Street, built in 1818 to the design of Thomas Hopper. The building was demolished in 1931.

Gardens pleasure grounds. (It is now in the Victoria and Albert Museum). Novello's abandoned these premises in 1965 but kept a publishing office at 27 Soho Square.

Soho's other musical institutions have included Charles Clagget's museum of musical instruments, which opened at 17 Greek Street in 1789; the Royal Society of Musicians, which had its headquarters in Lisle Street from 1808 to 1931; the Musicians' Union headquarters in Archer Street; and the London College of Music, which has been at 47 Great Marlborough Street since 1896.

ALL THAT JAZZ – AND ROCK 'N' ROLL

By the 1950s Soho could fairly claim to be the heart of London's contemporary music scene. The first jazz venue, Club 11, was established in 1948 at Mac's Club, on the corner of Archer Street and Great Windmill Street, by Ronnie Scott and John Dankworth. The same premises were later used by Cy Laurie's, which claimed a membership of almost seven thousand and was the first to offer seven sessions a week. In 1951 George Melly and Mick Mulligan organised the first all-nighter at the Mandrake in Meard Street, a chess club by day and an informal jam venue by night. In the same year Studio 51 opened at 19 Great Newport Street to offer New Orleans jazz. Humphrey Lyttleton played traditional jazz in an upstairs room in Leicester Square and modern jazz could be heard in the subterranean Metro in Old Compton Street, a favoured venue for French students. Ronnie Scott's was in Gerrard Street (moving to Frith Street in 1965). No. 44 Gerrard Street offered New Orleans jazz four times a week plus, on Tuesdays 'that jazz curiosity, Skiffle music.' Devotees of the latter could also patronise the Skiffle Cellar at 49 Greek Street.

The coffee-bars were nurseries of rock 'n' roll. Bruce Welch and Hank Marvin of The Shadows later claimed to have 'almost lived' at The Two I's' from April until September 1958, playing Buddy Holly and Everly Brothers numbers while waiting to be discovered - bolstered by the firm belief that 'If it was good enough for Tommy Steele it was good enough for us.' It was. Hank was heard and, with Bruce, marched round to Dean Street 'where we first met Cliff Richard, who was having a pink jacket fitted at the time.' The same coffee-bar was also the recruiting-ground for the two other 'Shadows', Jet Harris and Tony Meehan, as well as a crucial launch-pad for singer-actor Adam Faith and folk-singer-TV presenter Wally Whyton. In the following decade the crucial place was the Marquee, which moved from Oxford Street to 90 Wardour Street in 1964. Famed performers there included the Yardbirds, Manfred Mann, the Who, the Move, Jethro Tull, the Police, the Rolling Stones and Jimi Hendrix.

Shows and Spectacles

MRS CORNELYS AT CARLISLE HOUSE

Theresa Cornelys (née Imer, a.k.a. Pompeati, de Trenti and Rigerboos) (1723- 97) was a Viennese-born actress, singer, dancer and courtesan. Having married an Italian, lived with a Venetian senator, a German aristocrat and a wealthy Dutchman and given birth to two children (one allegedly fathered by Casanova), she settled in England in 1759 in the company of cellist and fraudster John Freeman (a.k.a. Fermor). Together they rented and refurbished Carlisle House in Soho Square and presented modest entertainments, consisting of dancing and card-playing, which were so instantly successful that an extension, consisting of a ballroom and a banqueting room, was built onto the back of the house so that more extravagant amusements could be offered.

Mrs. Cornelys' fabulous masquerades and top-quality concerts became the talk of the town. Entry by

Mrs. CORNELYS begs Leave to acquaint THE NOBILITY and GENTRY, *1763* SUBSCRIBERS to The SOCIETY in Soho-fquare, That the Eleventh Meeting will be Thurfday, May 5. Mrs. Cornelys alfo inform the Nobility and Gentry that have done her the Honour to fubfcribe this Year, that the next Year's Subfcription is now open, and thofe that will be fo good to continue their Favour, will, by fending for, have a printed Propofal given them. It is alfo defired that there be a Ball in favour of Mrs. Cornelys on Thurfday the 12th of May. Subfcriptions to be had at her Houfe in Soho-fquare by Subfcribers to the prefent Society, or by their Order.

132. A 1763 press advertisement to attract 'subscribers' to the assemblies at Mrs Cornelys' house in Soho Square.

subscription and prepaid ticket gave them a spurious air of exclusivity for they were soon grossly overcrowded. It soon became necessary for the hostess to require her guests to observe a one-way traffic system with respect to their sedan-chairs and carriages. Young Fanny Burney was dazzled by the decor and the company alike, but was appalled by the crush and the heat. Even the blasé Horace Walpole felt bound to

131. A scene at Mrs Cornelys.

133. *A mischievous caricature of Mrs Cornelys, published in 1776.*

134. *Admission ticket for a masquerade ball at Carlisle House. It cost 5 guineas for 'one gentleman or two ladies'.*

attend, if only to sneer at the 'fairy palace'. Recklessly extravagant and defiant of respectable opinion, Mrs. Cornelys inevitably made enemies, not least her creditors (including Chippendale, who supplied her furnishings) and the proprietors of rival attractions, notably the King's Theatre, Haymarket. When she began to put on unlicensed operatic performances the latter saw the chance to put her in court. Repeatedly fined, she battled on but the opening of the Pantheon (see pXXX) sealed her fate by luring away her remaining clientele and by October 1772 she was in prison for debt. Although she returned to the scene of her former glories five years later as manageress for its new owners, her decline was irreversible. A pathetic attempt to start up an asses' milk business in Knightsbridge got her on the wrong side of creditors again and she died in the Fleet Prison.

THE PANTHEON

The Oxford Street attraction which put Mrs Cornelys out of business was designed by architect James Wyatt, a resident of Newport Street, to function as a 'winter Ranelagh' pleasure garden. Its main room, a vast rotunda, was based on Santa Sophia in Istanbul, and surrounded with smaller rooms for cards, tea and supper. It took two and half years to build and the opening in January 1772 was attended by 1,500 guests. Horace Walpole thought it like 'Balbec in all its glory!' and the historian Edward Gibbon dubbed it the wonder of the century and the empire. Charles Burney outbid even these superlatives, calling it 'the most elegant structure in Europe, if not on the globe'. Such euphoria could not last. By 1780 the Pantheon was reducing its subscription rates and in 1791 it was converted into a theatre and less than a year later it was gutted by fire. Rebuilt by 1795, it broke its restorer, Crispus Clagett, and an attempt to establish it

135. *The interior of the Pantheon, the assembly rooms on Oxford Street.*

136. The Pantheon, Oxford Street – on the site of today's Marks and Spencer store.

as an opera house fell foul of the Lord Chamberlain. Stripped of its fittings in 1814, it was converted into a bazaar twenty years later, then taken over by Gilbey's the wine merchants. In 1937 it was bought and demolished by Marks and Spencer, whose store now occupies its site.

THE ARGYLL ROOMS

The Argyll Rooms, roughly at the unction of today's Regent Street and Great Marlborough Street, originated as the project of the feather-brained, but well-connected, Henry Francis Greville (1760-1816), an ex-army officer with a passion for amateur dramatics. Handsome, charming and devoid of business acumen, he borrowed heavily to buy the lease of a house in Little Argyll Street and then borrowed much more to refurbish it as a place of fashionable assembly. It opened in 1807 but the entertainments Greville offered proved amateurish and the would-be impresa-

rio was viciously lampooned by Byron. Broken in health, deserted by friends and hounded by creditors, Greville left England and died in Mauritius.

In 1813 the Argyll Rooms became a concert venue for the newly-established Philharmonic Society. In the same year Beau Brummell and three other dandies put on a ball there to celebrate recent successes at the gaming table; it was on this occasion that Brummell, who had fallen out with his former intimate, the Prince Regent, studiously ignored him and addressed his companion to deliver himself of the immortal line 'I say, Alvanley, who's your fat friend?'

During the construction of Regent Street in 1819 severe weaknesses were revealed in the building and Nash was obliged to undertake a complete rebuilding. Reopened in 1820 the Argyll Rooms witnessed memorable concert performances by Liszt (aged 12), Weber and Mendelssohn. After the building burned down in 1830 it was replaced by shops, which in 1919 were replaced by Dickins and Jones.

137. Another 'Argyll Rooms' had a brief existence near Piccadilly Circus, on the Trocadero site. Tennis courts there were converted into a venue for a circus (see illustration of 1837) and miscellaneous spectacles. A succession of theatrical ventures, and a reputation as a prostitutes' pick-up place, saw the building through to the end of the 19th century when it was bought up by J. Lyons & Co. for their Trocadero restaurant.

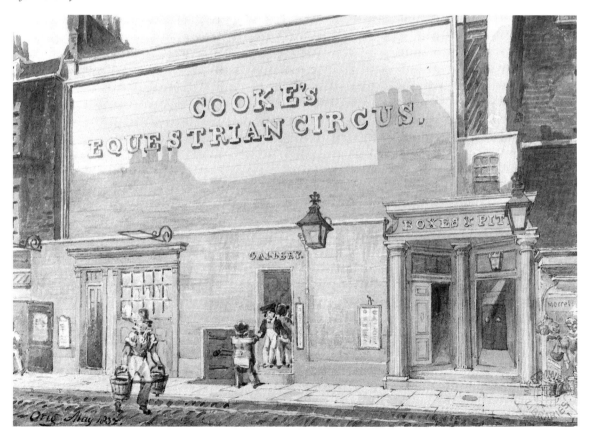

WOMBWELL'S MENAGERIE

The incompetent Greville's humble contemporary, George Wombwell, who kept a boot and shoe shop in Old Compton Street between 1804 and 1810, had all the entrepreneurial flair that Greville lacked. Starting with two snakes bought at a knock-down price, this rapacious, dwarfish drunk nevertheless managed to assemble three hugely successful menageries which travelled the length and breadth of England and made him a wealthy man by the time of his death in 1850.

THE PANORAMA

In 1787 Irish artist Robert Barker was granted a patent with the exclusive right to exploit for fourteen years his 'new contrivance or Apparatus which he calls La Nature a coup d'oeil for the purpose of displaying views of Nature at large by Oil painting...'.

Five years later he acquired a Leicester Square site, where he put up a circular building, ninety feet in diameter and fifty-seven feet high, to display his painted panoramas, the first being *A View of the Grand Fleet regularly moored at Spithead*. The venture proved so successful that Barker was soon able to buy out all his backers and to finance his son, Henry Aston Barker, to travel to Turkey and Paris to sketch new scenes. The battles of the Napoleonic wars, from the Nile to Waterloo, provided further spectacular subject-matter. *Waterloo* was such a hit that Henry, who had inherited the business on his father's death in 1806, was able to retire in 1826, handing the business over to his assistant John Burford and when *he* died the following year his brother, Robert, carried on, showing views of great cities such as Jerusalem and New York, and of stirring events such as the sieges of Sebastopol and Lucknow. Ruskin praised the Panorama as 'an educational institution of the highest and purest value... one of the most beneficial school instruments in London.' The business finally folded when the lease was acquired by the Marist Fathers to build a French Catholic church.

138. A section of Barker's rotunda in Leicester Place, 1801.

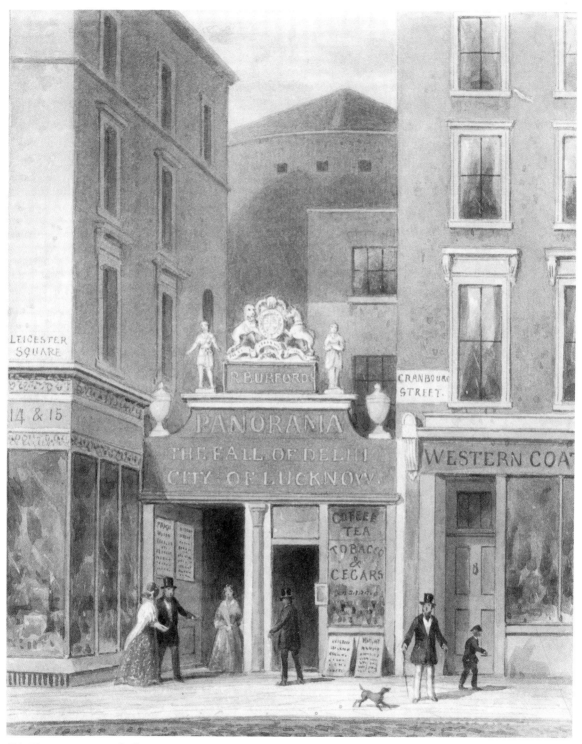

139. The entrance to Burford's Panorama in Cranbourn Street in 1858; by Thomas Hosmer Shepherd.

140. *The Sans Souci Theatre in Leicester Place on the left, and the east side of Leicester Square in the background, in 1816.*

SANS SOUCI

The demolition of Leicester House (see p25) made possible the erection of the ill-named Sans Souci Theatre. Its begetter was Charles Dibdin (1745-1814), a good actor and highly successful composer of patriotic and sentimental ballads but a quarrelsome man. The Sans Souci in Leicester Place was intended to be just as much his own as his shows were. It was thrown up in just twelve weeks, being only a front and back attached to the walls of existing houses on either side, and opened in October 1796. At first things seemed to go well but Dibdin was, within a few years, forced to mortgage it twice and finally closed it in 1805. Although elegantly fitted out, it was basically too small to be viable, although successive managements tried to find a niche market by putting on plays in foreign languages, or focusing on children's entertainment or hiring it out to amateur companies. (Edmund Kean as a boy gave acrobatic performances there.) In various non-theatrical incarnations the Sans Souci also served as an army clothier's warehouse, the annexe to a linen draper's, a restaurant and the Hotel de Versailles, before being demolished to make way for the Hotel de l'Europe, later the Victory Hotel. In 1922 it became an office-building for the NSPCC and was renamed Victory House.

141. Charles Dibdin

142. *The interior of the Sans Souci theatre.*

143. *James Wyld*

THE GREAT GLOBE

James Wyld (1812-87) MP and geographer, recog-
nised that the Great Exhibition of 1851 would flood
London with visitors who might well be tempted to
patronise other attractions, and determined to realise
a dream long contemplated, the construction of 'a
great model of the Earth's surface'. In return for a ten-
year lease he agreed with the Tulk family, who owned
the site, to build his model on the derelict gardens of
Leicester Square and then, at the end of his term, to
restore them to a decent condition. Not the least
attraction of the location must have been the proximity of the Panorama and the diverse attractions of
Savile House, which should surely bring in a healthy
passing trade. A hundred men worked round the
clock to build the Globe, which opened just a month
after the Crystal Palace, in June 1851. Over the course
of its existence it was used for a wide range of lectures
and exhibitions including a moving diorama of Russia and a mock-up of a gold-mine. After some legal
wrangling the building was demolished in 1862 and
the garden enclosed by a stone kerb and iron railing.
As a garden, however, it still left much to be desired
and the Metropolitan Board of Works threatened to
take it over. Further litigation blighted the area for

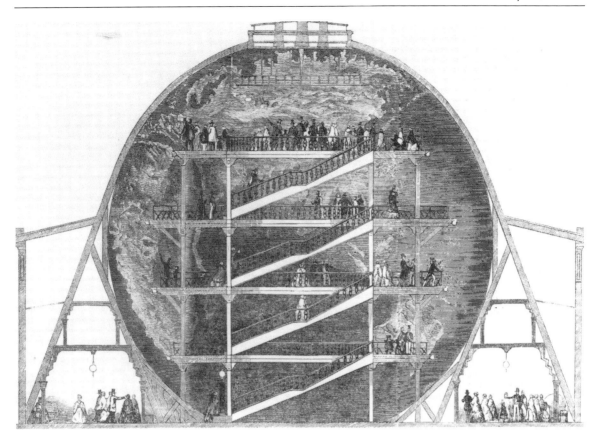

144. The interior of James Wyld's Great Globe in 1851.

145. Advertisement for the Great Globe.

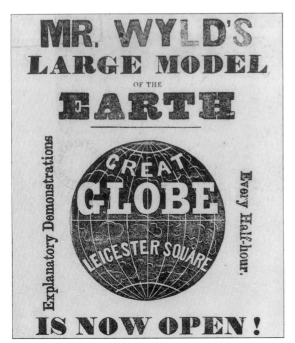

another decade until MP, financier and self-styled 'Baron' Albert Grant (1830-99) made a handsome offer to buy up the garden, restore it and give it to the Metropolis. Grant (born Gottheimer) specialised in prising funds from the proverbial widows and clergymen and in the course of a remarkable career raised some £24,000,000 – of which £20,000,000 was lost – for such ventures as Belgian Public Works, the Imperial Bank of China, Lima Railways and the Russian Copper Company. One of his most recent triumphs was the worthless Emma Silver Mine, for which he raised £1,000,000, pocketing £100,000 as 'promotion money'. But on this occasion Grant was, for once, as good as his word – or, rather, better – formally handing over the title-deeds to the Metropolitan Board of Works at the opening ceremony of the gardens on 3 July 1874. By 1879 he was totally bankrupt.

146. *The Great Globe in Leicester Square, from* The Builder, *April 1851.*

147. *The official handing over to the public of Leicester Square. From the* Illustrated London News, *July 1874.*

148. *'Baron' Albert Grant.*

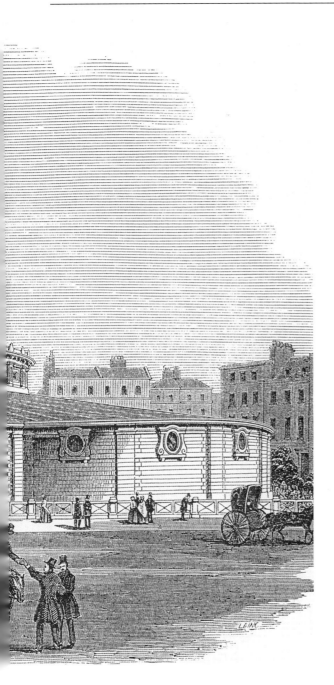

149. *The Royal Panopticon of Science and Art in Leicester Square; by Thomas Hosmer Shepherd.*

THE PANOPTICON

In February 1850 Edward Marmaduke Clarke, an Irish educationist, was granted a royal charter to establish the Royal Panopticon of Science and Art as 'an Institution for Scientific Exhibitions and for Promoting Discoveries in Arts and Manufactures', with himself as managing director. The idea, in brief, was to create a small scale, but permanent, version of the Great Exhibition which was to open shortly for six months in Hyde Park. Its council of management consisted of such worthies as the wealthy Quaker philanthropist Samuel Gurney, Peninsular War veteran General Sir John Wilson, a magistrate and an architect. The site for the new body was the eastern side of Leicester Square and the building, incorporating a vast hall, organ, galleries, lecture-rooms, offices and residential quarters, was built in the 'Saracenic' style, to inaugurate 'a new era in street architecture'. The internal decor incorporated an 'Ascending Carriage' (hydraulic lift), a fountain supplied by an artesian well beneath the premises, numerous copies of

famous sculptures and walls embellished with glass, mosaic, slate and alabaster. The front was covered with Minton tiles and the armorial bearings of such cultural icons as Purcell, Davy, Newton, Goldsmith, Herschel, Shakespeare, Watt and Bacon.

Within a month of its opening in March 1854 a thousand visitors a day were passing through the cast-iron portcullis which served as the building's main entrance. Regrettably the management was as dull and incompetent as the building was flamboyant. An outbreak of cholera that year kept visitors away from London. The entire venture soon collapsed, an unmitigated disaster.

In 1857 the Panopticon, which had cost an estimated £80,000, was auctioned off for £9,000 to E.T. Smith, a showman, who sold off the contents, installed a circus ring and reopened it in 1858 as the Alhambra Palace, presenting Howes and Cushing's American circus as its opening attraction. In 1861 it passed to William Wilde, who put on music hall, circus and dioramas and three years later Frederick

150. The proposed Royal Panopticon building dwarfed by a moorish dome. Illustrated London News, *January 1852.*

151. Advertisement for lurid entertainment at the Royal Panopticon.

152. Interior of the Royal Panopticon.

Strange, a caterer, took it over, spent £25,000 on refurbishment and introduced ballet, which was lavishly staged, if lamentably performed. A presentation of the 'Can Can' lost Strange his dancing licence in 1870 and he switched to concerts and comic opera.

In 1882 the theatre was largely destroyed by fire, although reconstruction preserved the original front, while enlarging the total capacity of the house to 4,000, including seating for 1,800. A new music and dancing licence was granted and ballet and music hall henceforth became the staple fare. The greatest successes of the revived theatre were *The Bing Boys are Here* (1916) in which George Robey achieved fame with *If You Were the only Girl in the World* and the Diaghilev Ballet season of 1919. In 1923 Gracie Fields attained stardom in the revue *Mr Tower of London*. The Alhambra was demolished in 1936 to make way for the Odeon cinema.

THE TROCADERO

In 1744 covered tennis-courts (for 'Real', not lawn, tennis) were erected on land adjacent to what had been Shaver's Hall (see p12). By the 1820s the tennis courts were being used as a circus, and an occasional theatre for displays of ventriloquism, conjuring and rope-dancing. Over the following century it served as a billiard-room, wax-works and theatre for farces, pantomimes and melodramas, under a wide variety of names. As the Argyll Rooms it became a notorious pick-up place for prostitutes. In 1882 it reopened as a music hall called the Trocadero Palace, where in 1886 Charles Coborn scored a huge hit with *Two Lovely Black Eyes*, a parody of a Christy Minstrel ballad. In 1895 J. Lyons & Co. converted the building to become a restaurant. It now houses the Guinness World of Records and other tourist attractions.

153. *The New Queen's Theatre, one of a succession of ventures on the site of the Trocadero.*

THE LONDON PAVILION

What is now the triangular corner site at the junction of Shaftesbury Avenue and Coventry Street has been associated with entertainment for two centuries. In 1797 Sir Henry Tichborne leased to Thomas Weeks, 'perfumer and Machinest', three houses here, plus a 'large Exhibition or Show Room', erected at the rear over the carriage-stabling in Black Horse Yard. Over a hundred feet long, with decor by the architect James Wyatt and the painter Biagio Rebecca, it featured a display of mechanical models, including a bird of paradise and a steel tarantula. This business died with Weeks in 1834 and the room was then used as a glass and china warehouse and an anatomical museum before being taken over by Loibl and Sonnhammer, who glassed over the adjacent courtyard and, gradually enlarging their holdings on the site, turned it into a sprawling entertainment and refreshment complex offering beer, coffee, tobacco, singers, a shooting-gallery and six American-style bowling alleys, the whole being grandly dubbed the 'London Pavilion'. The venture prospered mightily and in 1874 Loibl bought out his partner for £10,000, which Sonnhammer used to start Scott's fish restaurant in Coventry Street. It was at the London Pavilion, during the Russo-Turkish war of 1877, that G.H. Macdermott offered the first public rendition of *By Jingo*, a rousing xenophobic ballad which gave birth to the word 'jingoism'. The following year the Metro-

154. *The London Pavilion, Piccadilly Circus, before the 1885 rebuilding.*

155. The rebuilt London Pavilion in Piccadilly Circus; designed by R.J. Worley, 1885.

politan Board of Works decided to purchase the site to accommodate the general road realignment which led eventually to the creation of modern Piccadilly Circus and Loibl received the fabulous sum of £109,300 in compensation. The present London Pavilion, a total reconstruction, dates from 1885 and was built as 'the first music hall de luxe of the West End', clearly intended to outshine its neighbour and rival the Trocadero. It was subsequently the scene of emotional Suffragette rallies and extravagant C.B. Cochran musical reviews, before becoming a cinema in 1934. It now houses 'Rock Circus' and other tourist attractions.

THE HIPPODROME

The Hippodrome was built in 1899-1900 as a setting for 'a circus show second to none in the world, combined with elaborate stage spectacles impossible in any other theatre.' Designed by the doyen of theatre architects, Frank Matcham, it incorporated such special features as an arena which could serve as a circus ring with twelve-foot high steel railings or as a tank filled with 100,000 gallons of water.

In the first decade of its existence the Hippodrome featured shows with such extravagances as 'Redskins; shooting artificial rapids in canoes', twenty elephants (stabled in Lisle Street), seventy polar bears

and trained cormorants from China.

In 1909 extensive alterations were followed by a switch to variety and reviews and then, from 1926 onwards, musical comedies. In 1957 the Hippodrome was again totally remodelled to become The Talk of the Town, offering 'a complete evening's entertainment, consisting of dinner, dancing and a full variety show.'

It is now an amusement arcade.

THE PALLADIUM

Ugly, inconvenient Argyll House was bought and demolished in the 1860s by wine-merchant George Haig who built cellars, offices and a bazaar fronted with imposing Corinthian columns. When the latter failed it was converted to become the London base for Hengler's Circus from 1871 to 1895 and a skating rink from 1895 to 1899.

Attempts to revive it as a circus having failed, it was lavishly reconstructed in 1909-10 to the designs of Frank Matcham as the Palladium. In 1911 it witnessed the staging of the first Royal Command Performance and in the 1930s it was the home of the Crazy Gang. The tradition of children's entertainment established by its annual productions of J.M. Barrie's *Peter Pan* has been continued in the post-war period with spectacular Christmas pantomimes.

156. *A dramatic and no doubt exaggerated depiction of a production of* The Typhoon *at the London Hippodrome.*

Thespians and Theatres

THEATRICAL TEMPERAMENTS

Soho's proximity to Covent Garden, Drury Lane and Lincoln's Inn Fields long made it a convenient residence for 'theatricals'.

No. 37 Old Compton Street was built in 1728 and its first inhabitant was Thomas Walker. This was almost certainly the Soho-born actor who achieved huge acclaim as the first to play the leading male role, the highwayman Macheath, in John Gay's *The Beggar's Opera* which was first played in that same year. Walker was still there a decade later but after that faded into obscurity.

In 1740 Dublin-born Margaret (Peg) Woffington (c1714-60) established herself at 78 Dean Street. Sometime mistress of David Garrick (and simultaneously of the actor Charles Macklin), precocious, vivacious Peg excelled in saucy comedy but could play 'breeches parts' as well. On one occasion she bragged after a performance that half the men in the audience had mistaken her for one of their own sex – prompting a colleague to remark that any of the other men in the audience could convince them to the contrary. Hon-

oured by Garrick with the tuneful *My Lovely Peggy*, she also benefited much from his direction and prospered accordingly. By 1744 she had a country retreat at Teddington, as well as her Soho base. Her liaison with Garrick began to fade the following year and she moved out of Dean Street in 1748, returning to Dublin in 1750. She enjoyed tremendous success at Covent Garden after her return in 1754 but retired abruptly after collapsing on stage in 1757, unable to complete the prophetic line 'I would kiss as many .... '

No greater contrast with Peg Woffington could be imagined than the proper, indeed, prudish Sarah Siddons (1755-1831), who resided in unsullied propriety at 54 Great Marlborough Street from 1790 to 1804, when she was at the height of her fame. Born into the Kemble theatrical dynasty, she was without peer in tragic roles for thirty years. Hazlitt declared that 'in herself she is as great as any being she ever represented in the ripeness and plenitude of her power.' The personification of dignity in looks, voice and manner, she was all stage-presence – and a corresponding disappointment to her admirers in private conversation, acquiring a reputation for aloofness and avarice. Nevertheless she was appointed elocution tutor to the royal children. Herself a talented amateur sculptor, she was painted by Reynolds, Gainsborough and Lawrence, and honoured after her death with both a monument in Westminster Abbey and a statue at Paddington Green.

157. Peg Woffington.

158. Sarah Siddons; oil by George Romney.

159. Edmund Kean

160. William Macready

In 1820 Kemble's niece, Fanny (1809-93) came to live with her actor-manager father, Charles (1775-1854), then at 35 Gerrard Street, which she remembered as 'a handsome old house'. In 1829 she saved him from bankruptcy by making a stunning debut as Juliet at Covent Garden and went on to further triumphs by reviving a number of Mrs. Siddons' characteristic roles.

Deserted by his mother, Edmund Kean (1789-1833) was brought up by his uncle at 9 Lisle Street. His debut performance as Shylock in 1814 was a sensation and he remained unsurpassed in his portrayal of classic villains. Byron was awed by his Iago and Coleridge observed that 'to see him act is like reading Shakespeare by flashes of lightning.' Spell-binding on stage, he was consistently self-destructive when off it, and alcohol and syphilis hastened him to an early grave.

Kean's only serious rival was William Charles Macready (1793-1873), who lodged at 64 Frith Street at the time of his London debut in 1816 and lived at the same address from 1843 to 1851. His range was wider than Kean's and, unlike his chronically unpunctual rival, he was a stickler for rehearsal. Although his delivery was often mannered and unmusical his acute intellect ensured that he never spoke lines which he did not entirely understand. Macready was, however, more admired than loved, having an overbearing manner and an ungovernable temper.

RICHES AT THE ROYALTY

Dean Street was, for over a century, the site of a theatre whose significance was out of all proportion to its size. The *Survey of London* describes it discouragingly as 'small, obscurely sited, perilously combustible and rarely prosperous for long'.

It was built at the back of Nos. 73-4 Dean Street in 1834-7 by the leading theatrical architect of the day, Samuel Beazley, then resident at 29 Soho Square. The sponsor was a retired actress Fanny Kelly (1790-1882), occupant of No. 73, who had long dreamed of opening a drama school with its own theatre. The opening was, however, delayed until 1840 to accommodate some newfangled, prize-winning stage machinery which performed so disastrously when public performances did finally begin that the theatre closed within a week. Broken by ill-health and public ridicule, Miss Kelly allowed the theatre to be used from time to time by amateur groups. In 1845 a production of Ben Jonson's *Every Man in his Humour* was staged there, starring Charles Dickens. Passing through short-lived incarnations, it was served by such prodigious talents as Dion Boucicault, Ellen Terry and Charles Wyndham with only indifferent success. One shining exception was the premiere of Gilbert and Sullivan's *Trial by Jury* in 1875, which proved a triumph and ran for over three hundred performances. In the 1880s twice-yearly seasons of plays in French proved modestly successful.

161. *Fanny Kelly's Theatre in Dean Street.*

162. Mrs Kelly's theatre, now the Royalty, in 1882.

163. Mrs Kelly.

Subsequent celebrated premieres included Ibsen's *Ghosts* (1891), Brandon Thomas's *Charley's Aunt* (1892), Ibsen's *The Wild Duck* (1884) and Bernard Shaw's *You Never Can Tell* (1899). The Irish National Theatre Society made their first London appearance there in 1904, performing plays by Yeats and Synge. Later milestones included Noel Coward's *The Vortex* (1924) and Sean O'Casey's *Juno and the Paycock* (1925). By 1936 the danger of fire from celluloid-stores in adjacent properties brought the threat of final closure which came in 1938. A neo-Georgian office-block – Royalty House – was built on the site in the 1950s.

SHAFTESBURY AVENUE

Shaftesbury Avenue ranks with the Strand and St Martin's Lane as one of the capital's major theatrical thoroughfares. Completed in 1886, it saw the opening of its first, namesake theatre, in October 1888.

The Shaftesbury Theatre was built by John Lancaster, 'a shrewd Manchester merchant', to please his wife, the Shakespearean actress Ellen Wallis. Its first production, doubly appropriate on account of both his motive and her career, was *As You Like It*, though it was not until 1898 that the house enjoyed its first major success with *The Belle of New York*, which ran for 697 performances and revolutionised musical comedy in Britain. Five years later came *In Dahomey*, featuring the great novelty of an all-black cast over one hundred strong; it was extravagantly praised for 'its wonderful vitality, its quaint comedians, its catchy music and its unique environment'. In June of that year members of the cast were invited to Buckingham Palace to perform during a garden party held for the

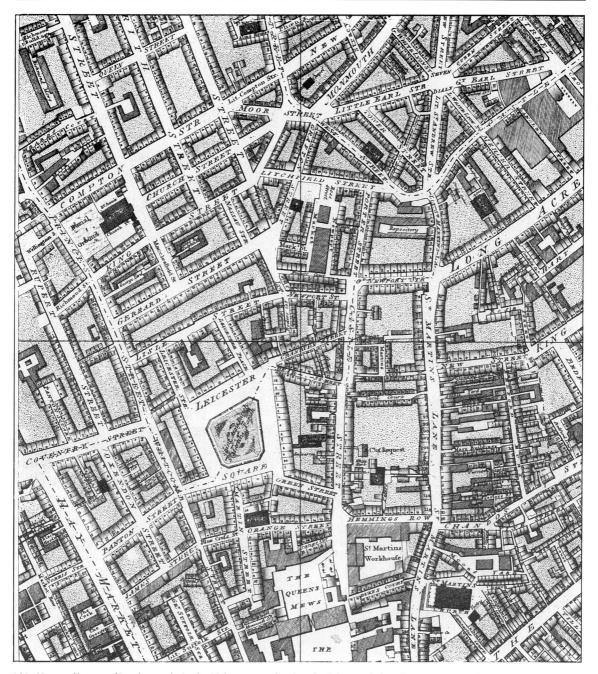

164. *Horwood's map of London early in the 19th century, showing the Soho area before the construction of Shaftesbury Avenue and Charing Cross Road.*

165. *The Palace Theatre in Cambridge Circus, just on completion in 1891.*

ninth birthday of Edward VII's eldest grandson, the future Edward VIII. Although the production was a sell-out, its exuberant dance novelty – 'the cakewalk' – was condemned by one critic as 'a grotesque, savage and lustful heathen dance, quite proper in Ashanti, but shocking on the boards of a London Hall.' In 1909 the Shaftesbury enjoyed another hit with *The Arcadians*. Later the theatre became a home of farce until it was blitzed out in 1941. It was not rebuilt and its name was appropriated by the Princes Theatre at the upper end of Shaftesbury Avenue.

The Shaftesbury's first rival was the Lyric, which opened in December 1888. Intended for comic opera, it disappointed its backers until 1910 when *The Chocolate Soldier*, a parody of Shaw's *Arms and the Man*. ran for over a year, much to Shaw's annoyance. Notable among its later productions were *Lilac Time* (1923-4), *The Winslow Boy* (1946) and *Irma La Douce* (1958-62).

The imposing Palace on Cambridge Circus was built by Gilbert and Sullivan impresario Richard D'Oyly Carte at the immense cost of £150,000 – more than seven times what it had cost to build the Shaftesbury. It was originally styled the 'Royal English Opera House' and opened in January 1891 with the premiere of Sir Arthur Sullivan's *Ivanhoe*. This was replaced with a French opera and then a short season of plays starring Sarah Bernhardt. But these pretensions to high culture proved disastrous and by December 1892 the new venture had metamorphosed into the 'Palace Theatre of Varieties'. Russian ballerina Anna Pavlova made her London debut here in 1910 but the theatre has enjoyed its greatest successes as a home to long-running musicals such as *No, No Nanette* (1925), *Song of Norway* (1946), *Sound of Music* (1961) and *Les Miserables* (1987).

The Apollo (1901) initially relied on musical comedy for its staple fare, then switched to serious drama, such as Sean O'Casey's *The Silver Tassie* (1929) and Terence Rattigan's *Flare Path* (1942) before finding its true metier with long runs of the sentimental *Seagulls over Sorrento* (1950), the farce *Boeing-Boeing* (1962) and Alan Bennett's satirical essay in pseudo-nostalgia *Forty Years On* (1968).

The adjoining Globe (1906) and Queen's (1907) were built by a boot-maker and an estate agent working in partnership. The Globe opened as the Hicks Theatre and starred veteran Seymour Hicks in its first production, but he soon disposed of his interest in the venture and in 1909 it changed its name to the Globe. Over the years the theatre became especially associated with the careers of Marie Lohr, Paul Scofield and Sir John Gielgud and in 1994 it was renamed in honour of Sir John. The Queen's staged the premieres of Shaw's *The Apple Cart* (1929) and Besier's *The Barretts of Wimpole Street* (1930) and an outstandingly successful series of classic plays under Gielgud (1937-8). Blitzed in 1940 it was not reopened until 1959.

166. *A typical Edwardian theatre programme issued by the Palace Theatre.*

The Prince Edward in Old Compton Street began life in 1930 as a theatre, opening with a musical comedy *Rio Rita*. In 1936 it was relaunched as a cabaret restaurant, the London Casino', and during the war it served as the Queensberry All-Services Club. In 1954 it became a cinema, pioneering widescreen Cinerama before reverting to theatrical status to stage Rice and Lloyd Webber's *Evita* and *Chess*.

Low Life

Soho's twentieth century reputation for vice and violence rests on a much greater historical continuity of the former than for the latter. Mayhem has been largely the work of non-residents and as far as murders go Soho appears to have no worse a record than its neighbours, glittering Mayfair or respectable Bloomsbury - though it has a couple of old examples, sufficiently colourful to be worthy of note.

In 1761 Anna Millicent King of 36 Leicester Square was murdered by her lodger, Swiss miniaturist Theodore Gardelle, who carried his taste for the miniature to a bizarre conclusion. Having disposed of her entrails 'in the boghouse', he subsequently 'carried bits of her about in parcels'.

In 1762 the Moroccan ambassador was living in Panton Square (demolished in the 1920s to make way for an extension to J. Lyons' Coventry Street Corner House). According to a contemporary account 'One of his attendants happened to displease him: he had him brought up to the garrett, and there sliced his head off.' This apparently pushed even Soho's traditional tolerance of foreign eccentricities too far and a mob allegedly broke into the ambassadorial residence 'demolished the furniture, threw everything they could lay their hands on out of the window, and threshed and beat the grand Moor and his retinue down the Haymarket.'

One of the area's earliest documented inhabitants, Anna Clarke, is described in 1641 as 'a lewd woman', but that was in the course of being arraigned for 'thretening to burne the houses at So : ho', for which she was merely bound over.

The first (1688) recorded occupant of 60 Frith Street was Elizabeth Price, 'a Player and mistress to several persons', who soon acquired a house in Pall Mall as well. Her affair with the fourth Earl of Banbury, a lethal duellist, ended in court after she claimed that he had married her in Verona. He denied the accusation and countered that she had engaged herself to a Spaniard with the singularly apt name of Don Hugo Simple. In 1697 the court decided that, if any form of marriage had taken place, it was bigamous on the Earl's part and therefore invalid anyway. Undaunted, Elizabeth Price, switched her tack to capitalise on her tangible assets and, still styling herself Countess, in 1689 contested a challenge to her right to mortgage the Frith Street property, which she had let to another notorious swordsman, Colonel John Beaumont. Unfortunately the outcome of this further confrontation remains undocumented.

Even less successful, but with apparently similar pretensions to grandeur, was Elizabeth Flint, who lived in a furnished room at 9 Meard Street in 1758. Renowned as 'generally slut and drunkard, occasion-

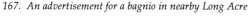

167. An advertisement for a bagnio in nearby Long Acre

168. Buskers in Leicester Square are not a recent phenomenon. This undated print, probably early 19th century, is entitled 'Harmony in Leicester Square', and depicts four groups of entertainers.

ally whore and thief', she was partially exonerated by her style. Even Dr Johnson noted that she had 'genteel lodgings, a spinnet on which she played and a boy that walked before her chair.'

Leicester Square, like nearby Covent Garden, was well known in the eighteenth century for its bagnios. Ostensibly a bath-house on the lines of a Turkish 'hammam', the bagnio also offered ancillary services similar in range to those available in its twentieth-century equivalent, the massage-parlour.

No. 27 Leicester Square, formerly the home of the Earl of Rockingham, was converted into a bagnio by one Roger Lacey around 1725/6. Very shortly afterwards the anatomist Nathaniel St Andre, a surgeon at the recently-established Westminster Hospital, used it as a convenient accommodation (presumably on the grounds that it offered a quasi-clinical setting) for the illiterate Mary Tofts, a Surrey woman, who claimed to have given birth to rabbits. S. Andre notified no less a person than the royal physician, Sir Hans Sloane, of her arrival 'at the bagnio in Leicester Fields, where you may if you please have the opportunity of seeing her delivered.' Mary Toft's fraud was deft enough to deceive both St Andre and Cyriacus Ahlers, George I's German surgeon, but was denounced after her examination by Sir Richard Manningham, the leading accoucheur of the day. Four days after her arrival in Leicester Fields she damned herself by being caught trying to procure rabbits rather than produce them.

After making a full confession, Mary, a mother of three, was briefly committed to Bridewell and then summarily dismissed to her native Godalming and her clothier husband. She was subsequently imprisoned for receiving stolen goods.

Hogarth, never one to miss a chance to cash in on free publicity, produced a satirical print, *Cunicularii*, whose title contained an obscure and obscene Latin pun. (His father was a schoolmaster who committed financial suicide by sinking his savings in a coffee-house where everyone was supposed to speak Latin.)

The brouhaha attending this ridiculous episode put people off eating rabbit for months but was evidently of considerable benefit in familiarising the public with the existence of the new bagnio, as it continued in that line of business under Lacey and a subsequent tenant, Skelton, until 1755.

From the Leicester Square bagnios the baton of vice went to the Hooper's Hotel at 21 Soho Square, on the corner with Sutton Street – which provided a discreet side entrance. Briefly the home of the Spanish ambassador (1772-5), it passed in 1778 into the charge of Thomas Hooper, who managed it as an hotel, while also providing visitors with the opportunity to gratify themselves in chambers variously entitled – the 'Painted Chamber', the 'Groto', the 'Skeleton Room' and the 'Coal Hole'. Clients included the Prince of Wales and the hotel's reputation apparently justified its inclusion in a treatise on *The Mysteries of Flagellation*.

169. An affray between well-heeled visitors to Leicester Square.

Leicester Square's reputation endured. In 1846 J.T. Smith commented that 'There is a considerable number of gaming-houses in the neighbourhood at the present time, so that the bad character of the place is at least two centuries old, or ever since it was built upon.' The 1886 edition of *Baedeker* warned readers that: 'The stranger is cautioned against going to any unrecommended house in Leicester Square, as there are several houses of doubtful reputation in this locality.'

In 1894 Mrs Ormiston Chant and her Purity Campaign conducted a sustained crusade of vilification against the Empire (see p25), a notorious promenade for prostitutes. Twenty-year-old Winston Churchill, a Sandhurst cadet, took a leading role in the opposition to her efforts, his first foray into public controversy. In a letter to the *Westminster Gazette*, he argued that: 'the improvement in the standard of public decency is due rather to improved social conditions and to the spread of education than to the prowling of prudes...Nature metes out great and terrible punishments to the 'roué and libertine' - far greater punishments than it is in the power of any civilised State to award. These penalties have been exacted since the world was young, and yet immorality is still common. State intervention, whether in the form of a Statute or by the decision of licensing committees,

will never eradicate the evil.... whereas the Vigilante Societies wish to abolish sin by Act of Parliament, and are willing to sacrifice much of the liberty of the subject into the bargain, the 'anti-prudes' prefer a less coercive and more moderate procedure.'

A fortnight later Churchill assigned himself a starring role in a dramatic last-ditch effort to rally the anti-prudes and wrote to his brother excitedly about what he had done :-

'Did you see the papers about the riot at the Empire last Saturday? It was I who led the rioters - and made a speech to the crowd... "Ladies of the Empire, I stand for Liberty!... You have seen us tear down these barricades tonight. See that you pull down those who are responsible for them at the coming election."'

The author of these exuberant lines was ironically unaware that, even as he wrote them, his father was succumbing to the last ravages of syphilis.

The 'anti-prudes' lost their campaign, as the newly-established London County Council insisted, as a condition of renewing the theatre's music and dancing licence, that the notorious promenade area be altered to frustrate soliciting.

The Empire subsequently moved forward into a new era of uplifting balletic spectacle under the gracious influence of Adeline Genée.

Somewhere to Eat

Soho largely catered for its own until just over a century ago, when a journalist wandered into Kettner's, found the food excellent, the service pleasing and the bill surprisingly moderate. Moved to share his good fortune with his countrymen, he wrote an article for *The Times*. Kettner's was made. Within a decade the Austrian founder, formerly chef to the French Emperor, Napoleon III, had become a metropolitan institution. *Kettner's Book of the Table* was looked on as *the* work of reference in culinary matters and his restaurant became one of Oscar Wilde's most favoured. Could one ask more?

Kettner's was founded in 1868. Maison Bertaux in Greek Street claims to be London's oldest French patisserie, dating from 1871 and Gennaro's at 44 Dean Street claimed to be the first Italian restaurant in Soho and to have numbered among its customers Enrico Caruso, Dame Nellie Melba and the kings of Greece, Siam and Yugoslavia. Its site has, since 1985, been occupied by the Groucho Club.

By 1886 Baedeker's guide-book to London was assuring its readers that 'there are many cheap and good foreign restaurants in Soho' and recommending no less than ten of them, including Chiale's at 20 Leicester Square ('French cuisine and attendance, moderate charges'); the Wedde at 12 Greek Street ('German house'); Blanchard's at 5 Beak Street ('ladies not after 5 p.m. Good wines'); Maison Dorée in Glasshouse Street ('elegantly fitted up') and, of course, Kettner's.

Soho's gastronomic move up-market was signalled by the construction in 1889 of the purpose-built Pelican Club on the site of 34/35 Gerrard Street; alas, only to go bankrupt within three years and make way for a telephone exchange. L'Escargot, established around 1900 by Georges Gaudin, took its motto from its snail mascot - 'slow but sure', a formula which may well have assisted its survival into the era of 'fast food'. In 1915 Ciro's of Deauville opened a luxurious new dining-club in Orange Street; an ironic fate decreed that it should subsequently house the University of London's School of Dental Surgery. The vigorous theatre-building boom of the turn of the century brought Soho restaurants an additional market among theatre-goers. By the inter-war period Soho dining

170. Blanchard's Restaurant in Beak Street, c1890.

171. *An evening of Table D'Hôte at the Trocadero.*

172. *L'Escargot restaurant in Greek Street. The old emblematic plaque of the proprietor riding on a snail shown here is now inside the building.*

had begun to secure its place in popular fiction. Agatha Christie's Hercule Poirot and Captain Hastings become regular devotees of (unspecified) small Soho restaurants. Dorothy L. Sayers actually was a regular patron of the Moulin d'Or at 27 Romilly Street and made it the model for 'Au Bon Bourgeois' in *Unnatural Death*. Her fictional hero Lord Peter Wimsey dines (dreadfully) at the mythical Soviet Club in Gerrard Street, which was based on the Detection Club, which did meet at No. 31 and of which she was a luminary.

A 1924 London guide-book listed more than two dozen Soho restaurants, though noting somewhat sniffily that 'of late years the inexpensive restaurants of Soho have enjoyed an extraordinary vogue, and this fact seems to have somewhat modified the previously exclusive foreign air of the district.' In Dean Street Quo Vadis took over Karl Marx's former home in 1926. Wheeler's began as a retail oyster shop in 1929; by the 1950s it offered the discerning palate thirty-two different ways of serving sole and lobster. Despite the fact that it was emphatically not a Chinese restaurant, it had become traditional that almost all of its kitchen staff were.

A 1956 guide listed over three dozen Soho restaurants, including eight Italian, five French, four Chinese, three 'French and Italian', three Hungarian, two Indian, two Spanish and two fish specialists - one of which also served meat-dishes, but in a side-room. There were also one each of Swedish, Austrian, Portuguese and Turkish, the last claiming tentatively to be 'the only purely Turkish restaurant, we believe, in England.' The specialities on offer ranged from Kashmiri pilau to Tripes a la mode de Caen, from Lobster Newburgh to Ravioli al Sugo. L'Escargot, The Gay Hussar and Le Versailles all unashamedly described their menus as 'Expensive', while Kettner's acknowledged itself to be 'Far from cheap'. Gennaro's warned that it was 'Not recommended for those on a reducing diet', while the Hong Kong reassured the querulous 'Leave the choice to the waiter if you're in doubt.' Petit Savoyard boasted of its 'lounge bar decor and mural by Maurice Rickards' but the Majorca Spanish Restaurant contented itself with merely being 'nicely decorated'. Casa Pepe offered instruction in drinking Spanish wine from a 'porron' - an earthen pitcher held at arm's length. Tyrol offered the less testing challenge of zither music. At Tre Kronor

173. Waiters and waitresses line up for the start of the 1994 Soho Waiters' Race, an event organised by the Soho Restaurateurs Association as part of the annual Soho Festival.

customers could place themselves with confidence in the hands of 'M. Andre, a restaurateur who served Scandinavian royalty', while at Ley On's Chop Suey they could revel in the company of the ebullient proprietor 'a part-time film actor and an enthusiastic race-horse owner'. Chez Vatel claimed the self-evidently discerning patronage of 'TV and French clientele', only to be up-staged by Isow's 'large visiting Hollywood clientele'.

A decade later *The New London Spy: A Discreet Guide to the City's Pleasures* could assert without qualification that:

'Soho is the traditional restaurant centre in London... Traditional restaurants which... still serve decent meals with professional waiters, clean tablecloths and cutlery, are no longer fashionable but still provide the most consistent value for money.'

Indeed, the *Spy* recommended any Soho establishment 'where a chasseur can be seen in a brightly-coloured soup-stained uniform looking around helplessly for taxis.'

In November 1968 the *Sunday Times*, noting that Soho had 165 restaurants and 78 pubs, conducted a survey of who was lunching where on a single Friday. Jonathan Miller was being treated by the editor of *Vogue* at the Trattoria Terrazza; publisher Andre Deutsch and journalist James Cameron were at the Gay Hussar; Professor Cecil Day Lewis was at L'Epicure, film-star James Robertson-Justice was at Wheeler's, newspaper tycoon Cecil King was at Quo Vadis and the film-making Boulting brothers were at Au Jardin des Gourmets.

Floreat Soho

by Bryan Burrough,
Chairman of the Soho Society

Soho survived three centuries of change and Hitler's bombs only to be threatened with total annihilation in the 1960s. The threat was called 'comprehensive redevelopment' and entailed the demolition of most of Soho. Pedestrian walkways, even helipads, were planned. Piccadilly Circus would receive particularly thorough treatment: between three and four hundred thousand square feet of offices in blocks twenty to thirty storeys high, six lanes of traffic whizzing through it at ground level and ordinary people sixty feet up in the air sharing concrete walkways with windblown rubbish. Vigorous lobbying by the Save Piccadilly Campaign alerted politicians and the public to the insanity of the Piccadilly Circus proposals, which were finally abandoned by Westminster City Council in 1974.

Soho itself still bore the signs of war. Bomb-sites existed in Old Compton Street, Newport Place, Shaftesbury Avenue and Great Marlborough Street and the bombed site of the parish church of St Anne was a temporary car park – a use described in 1956 by the churchwarden, one Miss Dorothy L. Sayers, as an insult to the people of Soho. There were also slum-clearance sites in Peter Street, Marshall Street, Livonia Street and St Anne's Court. The population was decreasing to the extent that the Soho Parish School in Great Windmill Street had only sixty children on the roll and looked likely to close. Conversely, Soho's restaurants were flourishing again and hundreds of craftsmen were kept busy – tailors, theatrical costumiers, silversmiths, clockmakers, violin makers, gun makers and, in Golden Square, the ostrich feather curlers and trimmers (for the chorus girls). The boot last-makers in Meard Street and George Benford & O'Shea (horological sundriesmen to the Trade) were both still taking on apprentices. The high quality products of Soho's craftsmen were sold through the prestige shops of Regent Street and St James's and through Savile Row tailors.

But the observant visitor in the late 1960s would detect problems. Those who had assembled property portfolios during and after the War in anticipation of comprehensive development let their properties on leases with six-month break clauses. This allowed the landlord to get rid of a tenant and demolish a building quickly if the need arose. The industry best placed to accept these terms was, of course, the sex industry, better known in Soho as 'the Vice'. Unlike restaurants which require heavy investment in equipment, the Vice could flit from shop to shop as they became available. Corruption in the Metropolitan Police

allowed the Vice to become established in the 1960s and early 1970s. Yet ironically, when senior police officers were gaoled in 1974, the Vice was then left unchecked and still under the control of its former owners, though now in prison.

Soho, in these circumstances, appeared to be exempt from laws which applied elsewhere and when, in October 1972, local councillor Thelma Seear called a public meeting in Kettner's Restaurant she could have had little idea of the consequences that would follow. Instead of a few local worthies she faced a room packed wall to wall with Sohoites – very angry at what was happening in the neighbourhood.

The Soho Society was founded at that meeting, its aims 'to make Soho a better place in which to live, work or visit'. With widespread support it took the new Society only a few months to persuade the Westminster City Council to declare most of Soho a Conservation Area – thus ending the threat of widespread demolition. The Society turned its attention to community activities, reinforcing links between residents and business concerns. The annual Soho Festival, with its now famous waiters' race, started in 1974. A Chamber Orchestra, a Local History Group, a soccer tournament and many other social activities followed, including a newspaper – the *Soho Clarion* – with a circulation of 7,000 copies.

Soho faced two major problems – the Vice, which a Society survey in 1978 revealed to be operating in 185 buildings, and a lack of housing. The Vice gave Soho a reputation for violence and exploitation and tourists were increasingly complaining of being mugged of cash in these establishments or of being cheated.

The Society decided to take on the Vice and twenty-three Public Enquiries into illegal use followed – the Society won them all. This encouraged the Society to lobby for the licensing of sex shops and control over the sex industry and after a long campaign, new laws were introduced in 1984. As a consequence, in the next few years the number of buildings used by the Vice fell from about 185 to about 20.

However, without housing the Soho community was doomed and in 1976 members of the Society founded the Soho Housing Association with £700 and the use of St Anne's Church Tower as a headquarters: it is now worth over £40 million and has more than 400 flats in the West End. A happy consequence is that the Parish School, no longer in danger of closure, is full with 136 children on the books, plus two day nurseries both also full.

The Society acted as the catalyst to redevelop the site of St Anne's church, bringing together the various parties and helping to produce an award-winning scheme which includes not only housing, but a new church, a community centre, a headquarters for the Society and space for a proposed Museum of Soho. The church was consecrated on St Anne's Day, 1991.

174. *The boot and shoe last-maker's workshop in Meard Street.*

So, whither Soho? There is today a new café society downing cappuccinos on pavements despite the traffic fumes. Soho has suddenly become a centre of gay pilgrimage – Pink Soho. But although the recession seems to have ended in Soho, a third of Soho's floorspace is still empty – just look at the upper floors. Most of the craftsmen have gone, not because of the recession but as a consequence of legislation which increased the rents of workshops.

But Soho will survive. The restaurants are busy. It is a very good place in which to live – safe, friendly, with good schools and shops. Recently significant areas of offices have been changed back to residential use. A development of 61 flats in Wardour Street was completely sold before the flats were even built. The Soho air is still perfumed with the smell of roasting coffee and with croissants coming out of the ovens at 9.30 in the morning. The chimes of the parish clock still ring out over Soho rooftops as they have since 1691. Some will complain that Soho isn't what it was, but in the words of the late Ian Board of the Colony Room, it probably never was anyway.

175. The informality of St Anne's Court in the 1920s.

Further Reading

Asa Briggs: *Karl Marx in London: An Illustrated Guide* (BBC 1982)

Clergy of St Anne's: *Two Centuries of Soho, Its Institutions, Firms and Amusements* (Truslove & Hanson 1898)

Simon Dewes: *Soho* (Rich & Cowan 1952)

Daniel Farson: *Soho in the Fifties* (Michael Joseph 1987, Pimlico 1993)

Yves Jaulmes: *The French Protestant Church of London and the Huguenots* (French Protestant Church of London 1993)

Charles Lethbridge Kingsford: *The Early History of Piccadilly, Leicester Square and Soho* (Cambridge University Press 1925)

Tessa Murdoch: *The Quiet Conquest: The Huguenots 1685 to 1985* (Museum of London 1985)

Nikolaus Pevsner: *The Buildings of England, London I : The Cities of London and Westminster* (Penguin Books 1957)

E.F. Rimbault: *Soho and its Associations* (Dulau 1895)

Ann Saunders: *The Art and Architecture of London: An illustrated guide* (Phaidon Press second ed. 1988)

J.T. Smith: *Nollekens and His Times* (Century Hutchinson 1986)

Judith Summers: *Soho: A History of London's Most Colourful Neighbourhood* (Bloomsbury Publishing 1989)

Sir John Summerson: *Georgian London* (Penguin, revised 1978)

Survey of London (ed. F.H.W. Sheppard):
  Vols XXXI & XXXII The Parish of St. James, Westminster (Athlone Press 1963)
  Vols XXXIII & XXXIV The Parish of St. Anne, Soho (Athlone Press 1966)

Edwin Webb: *Literary London : An Illustrated Guide* (Spellmount Ltd 1990)

George Williams: *Guide to Literary London* (Batsford 1973)